CREATING THE
PERFECT PATIO

CREATING THE
PERFECT PATIO

HOW TO DESIGN AND PLANT AN OUTSIDE SPACE, WITH PRACTICAL ADVICE AND 550 INSPIRING STEP-BY-STEP PHOTOGRAPHS

JOAN CLIFTON AND JENNY HENDY

southwater

This edition is published by Southwater, an imprint of Anness Publishing Ltd, Blaby Road, Wigston, Leicestershire LE18 4SE

info@anness.com;
www.southwaterbooks.com;
www.annesspublishing.com

If you like the images in this book and would like to investigate using them for publishing, promotions or advertising, please visit our website www.practicalpictures.com for more information.

Publisher: Joanna Lorenz
Editorial Director: Helen Sudell
Project Editor: Emma Clegg
Designer: Abby Franklin
Practical photography: Howard Rice
Illustrator: Robert Highton
Production Controller: Bessie Bai

A CIP catalogue record for this book is available from the British Library.

Previously published as part of a larger volume, *The Complete Practical Guide to Patio, Terrace, Backyard & Courtyard Gardening*

ETHICAL TRADING POLICY
At Anness Publishing we believe that business should be conducted in an ethical and ecologically sustainable way, with respect for the environment and a proper regard to the replacement of the natural resources we employ.

As a publisher, we use a lot of wood pulp in high-quality paper for printing, and that wood commonly comes from spruce trees. We are therefore currently growing more than 750,000 trees in three Scottish forest plantations: Berrymoss (130 hectares/320 acres), West Touxhill (125 hectares/305 acres) and Deveron Forest (75 hectares/185 acres). The forests we manage contain more than 3.5 times the number of trees employed each year in making paper for the books we manufacture.

Because of this ongoing ecological investment programme, you, as our customer, can have the pleasure and reassurance of knowing that a tree is being cultivated on your behalf to naturally replace the materials used to make the book you are holding.

Our forestry programme is run in accordance with the UK Woodland Assurance Scheme (UKWAS) and will be certified by the internationally recognized Forest Stewardship Council (FSC). The FSC is a non-government organization dedicated to promoting responsible management of the world's forests. Certification ensures forests are managed in an environmentally sustainable and socially responsible way. For further information about this scheme, go to www.annesspublishing.com/trees

PUBLISHER'S NOTES
Although the advice and information in this book are believed to be accurate and true at the time of going to press, neither the authors nor the publisher can accept any legal responsibility or liability for any errors or omissions that may have been made nor for any inaccuracies nor for any loss, harm or injury that comes about from following instructions or advice in this book.

Great care should be taken if you include pools, ponds or water features as part of your garden landscape. Young children should never be left unsupervised near water of any depth, and if children are able to access the garden all pools and ponds should be fenced and gated to the recommended specifications.

CONTENTS

INTRODUCTION

The patio has tremendous potential to increase the quality of our lives in over-populated living spaces. We all benefit from a place to escape outdoors, somewhere with natural elements away from the everyday hubbub and the noise and pollution around us. Whether you have a small hard-landscaped area or a more extensive paved space, there are endless ways to bring it to life.

Above: *Pale decking, bold partitions and raised planters create a clean, modern patio.*

The patio that you choose will depend on many factors, from its size, aspect and soil quality to your own ideas about visual styles and planting preferences. This book investigates various style options for a contained outside area. Each section looks at one of six generic approaches to patios and courtyards – Traditional Lines; Mediterranean Warmth; Living Outdoors; The Edible Garden; A Peaceful Oasis; and Modern Spaces. The same elements within each – approaches to flooring, walls and screens, plants and containers, structures and furniture, ornament and water features, and lighting – are explored and assessed for suitability, with integrated step-by-step features showing useful techniques.

Traditional Lines is the natural choice of those who respect orderly proportions and classical features. Mediterranean Warmth offers charming patios, bright colours, captivating scents and the promise of long, sunny days outside. Living Outdoors explores a concept that makes your patio a real-life living space, with interior styling, and a place to cook, eat, relax, welcome friends, bathe and sleep. The Edible Garden shows the potential of a decorative kitchen garden in which to cultivate fresh vegetables as well as

fruit and flowers for the table. For those who would like to escape the urban bustle, A Peaceful Oasis demonstrates how to create a calm, private paradise. The chapter on Modern Spaces looks at minimal, streamlined spaces using contemporary and experimental materials, or traditional materials that are combined with a modern twist.

The techniques are chosen for their relevance to the chapter, but many of them are interchangeable – such as laying random paving,

painting a rendered wall, planting clematis against trellis, lighting a pathway and pruning bamboo.

Finally, a section on Maintaining your Patio shows how to keep your space at its best, ranging from plant upkeep and pruning and training to watering techniques and seasonal jobs.

The patio is a garden in miniature. It gives the opportunity to enact any decorative or horticultural fantasy, classical or romantic, productive or spare. So use the ideas here to create something special of your own.

Left: *The view through a trained evergreen archway gives a tempting glimpse of the visual texture that lies beyond.*

Right: *A bed of alliums and astilbe mirrors the colours in the partitions behind.*

TRADITIONAL LINES

A patio or courtyard using a traditional approach will work along established guidelines and will create an experience of formality, elegance and serenity. Taking as its inspiration the classical French and Italian gardens of the 17th and 18th centuries, this style feels familiar and reassuring. Composed of clean, symmetrical lines, this outside space is laid out with care and evokes calm and order. Fine specimen plants, elegant ornaments and imposing architectural features reinforce the theme, bringing their own distinct finishing touches.

The restricted space in a patio lends itself to this formal approach, the style working effectively within the contained boundaries. In contrast with the demands of larger gardens, its manageable scale permits a scheme that can be both impressive and dramatic, without being overly expensive.

Left: *The interlocking lines of this box-edged parterre perfectly complement the elegantly executed paving design. The complex lattice pattern is achieved by contrasting differently coloured pavers against a stone and textured gravel background.*

FLOORING FOR TRADITIONAL SPACES

The hard landscaping of a patio or courtyard will form the structural elements of the design. In a traditional-style garden, flooring might range from cobbles and flagstones to timber and brick, and each of these materials acts as the consistent element on to which all the other details are imposed.

Above: *The random shapes of smooth, washed pebbles are used in a curved path.*

Matching the Style

A successful patio design must reflect its surroundings. To create an intelligent, elegant and well-executed scheme you should consider the architectural qualities of the setting together with the character and scale of the adjacent landscape. Therefore, your design approach should take into account the type, colour and texture of surrounding materials. If buildings are constructed from brick, is it coloured red or yellow? Is it bright and new or old and worn? If the buildings are made from stone, is the tone predominantly yellow or grey? Are wall finishes rendered with cement or are they painted? Are there any significant elements of colour or material that could be picked up on or mirrored in other selected features?

Above: *Low brick retaining walls allow planting to integrate naturally into this shallow flight of steps.*

Choice of Materials

It is important to understand what your options are and the qualities of different materials. Traditional designs tend to utilize natural materials. Stone, which is a fundamental element of landscape work, varies hugely in colour, texture and durability depending on its composition. In addition, its appearance can be altered dramatically by how it is cut and finished. Stone pavers, for example, can be 'sawn' to produce a crisp, square edge and smooth finish, resulting in a fresh, new appearance. An order for 'riven' flags will produce an uneven surface and edges, which suggest age.

Put simply, the way different stones have evolved can be described in three textural types: soft, hard and flaky. Soft stones include sandstone, which normally occurs in yellowish tones and the

Above: *Wooden planks are cut into short lengths and used to create an informal deck that follows the intersections of the garden and creates a seating area.*

more whitish/grey-toned limestone. Reference is frequently made to 'York stone', a type of sandstone that comes from the north of England. It has a beautiful honeyed colour and a smooth texture that blends well with brick-built surroundings. It is one of the most superior paving materials.

The hardest stone of all is granite. It is supremely hardwearing and completely non-porous. But, as a result, it is difficult and time consuming to work, and thus expensive. The highly polished finish frequently seen in corporate settings is seldom appropriate in a domestic situation. Textured surfaces, achieved by hammering or burning the surface,

fit better with nature and are much easier on the eye. Granite should be employed with care because its somewhat 'aggressive' appearance can look too harsh in a garden.

Granite is perhaps most useful in the form of small cubes, or 'setts', which are extremely effective in making paths and steps. Order them with a textured, non-slip surface. They are easy to handle and lend themselves well to curvy designs. They are also very well suited to edging details for paths and steps and they make an effective device for forming a border around a tree or planting bed.

Limestone, which frequently contains fossils that add immensely to the beauty of the stone, is more fragile, or flaky, than granite. Most crucially, it is porous and has a tendency to stain, often from the feet of furniture or other objects placed on it. Tannins can leach from insufficiently matured timber

furniture, especially oak, while steel, even though protected, will rust sooner or later. It is therefore perhaps best used in locations used exclusively for foot traffic, such as paths and steps.

Below: *Moulded paving slabs in complementary honeyed tones.*

Above: *Pale-coloured materials introduce a calm, tranquil ambiance. Natural limestone slabs occur as plinths to the retaining walls and as contrast elements of texture and shape in a path of small paving setts.*

Below: *Gentle flights of steps descend to an elegant patio of pale granite paving, the central detail using contrasting dark stone.*

LAYING BRICK PAVERS

If they are chosen with care, concrete pavers that have been formed to look like house bricks are a practical and attractive choice for the traditional garden. Look for rustic, brindled or antique-effect bricks. It is not always necessary to lay them in a bed of concrete. They can be simply laid in a sand base with sand-filled joints – these allow rainwater to percolate, reducing the risk of flooding after a heavy shower.

1 Excavate the area to be paved and prepare a sub-base of about 5cm (2in) of compacted hardcore or sand-and-gravel mix. This prevents sunken areas developing at a later date. Set an edging along one end and side first. Check that it's level and then mortar it into position, laying the pavers as shown.

2 Lay a 5cm (2in) bed of sharp sand over the compacted hardcore. Then, using a straight-edged piece of wood notched at the ends to fit over the edging bricks, scrape off surplus sand. This method provides a consistently level surface on which to bed the remaining bricks.

3 Position the pavers in your chosen design, laying about 2m (6ft) at a time. Make sure they butt up to each other tightly and are firm against the edging. Mortar further edging strips into place as you proceed. On a slope, work upwards from a solid edging to prevent slippage.

4 Hire a flat-plate vibrator to consolidate the bricks on the sand base. To avoid damage, do not go too close to an unsupported edge with the vibrator. Alternatively, especially in small areas, tamp the pavers down with a club hammer used over a piece of wood to prevent chipping.

5 Brush loose sand into the joints of the pavers with a broom, then vibrate or tamp again. It may be necessary to repeat the vibrating process once more to achieve a firm, neat finish. The patio is then ready to use. Brush in more sand later to prevent moss and weeds growing.

GETTING CREATIVE

• *You can lay bricks, brick pavers or cube-shaped setts (terracotta/clay, granite or the cheaper concrete reproductions) in a wide range of patterns and designs. If you are working on a larger area, which could become monotonous if paved using just a simple pattern, it is best to try new combinations.*

• *Smaller, square-shaped setts are the most versatile to use, but both bricks and setts can be worked in as panels between stone or reproduction paving slabs, or to form a smart edging or border.*

• *Because of their small size and proportion, setts and bricks are useful for creating complex formal designs for curved paths, circular patios and focal point details.*

Right: *Red terracotta quarry tiles provide a warm and welcoming background for this roof-top garden.*

Visual Dynamics

The physical qualities of building materials play important sensory and directional roles in the design process. A rise of granite steps could provide a solid ascent to a terrace above a soft grassy lawn, while narrow borders of black slate would emphasize the route of a pale flagstone path. This balance of soft and hard, dark and light can be used to create exciting visual and tactile effects. Avoid polished surfaces, which are less suited to domestic landscapes, appearing overly formal. The subtler character of textured finishes is easier on the eye and more in tune with the qualities of foliage and stems.

Having terrace areas for seating and dining is important in a courtyard, offering a space for relaxation and entertainment. To develop the full potential of a plot, look at incorporating three-dimensional devices, such as an above-ground fountain. It may be possible to create a secondary garden level beyond the terrace. Raised planting beds contained within retaining walls are a good way to achieve this.

Above: *Random shaped slabs make it easy to deal with curved paving features.*

The walls create a background for the terrace, and provide support for the upper garden. You would also need to have a flight of steps. Such works are not minor, but the bonus of working on a relatively small area is that your budget can go further.

Juxtaposing Materials

When designing flooring, a simple approach is best. The use of lots of different materials and textures results in a visual chaos that reduces the feeling of space. So select one main material to create a neutral background and use it throughout. To reinforce the layout and bring the design into focus, use a contrasting material to create the finishing details. Border edgings prevent paths appearing to 'drop off' into the garden and can play an important safety role on steps.

You could use reclaimed handmade bricks (normally too soft and crumbly to be used as paving in its own right) as detailing. Combined with the warm tones of a sandstone path, it would make an excellent visual connection with a brick-built house. Alternatively, engineering brick is durable and well suited to paving. While it looks most at home in a modern setting, it has its place in certain types of traditional gardens, especially urban ones.

Slate is a beautiful, soft-looking stone; it ranges in colour through soft greens and mauves, and almost to black. Slate is elegant when used as detailing in combination with cool-looking limestone surfaces. Its texture and colour varies and the brighter shades can be used as inserts to liven up plain paving.

Environmental and social factors to do with the choice of materials can result in a dilemma between the constraints of budget and the concerns of conscience. Because the quarrying and finishing of stone is highly labour intensive, it is sourced from regions where labour costs are low. So when ordering materials find out if the source is sustainable and that fair practices are in operation.

WALLS AND SCREENS FOR TRADITIONAL SPACES

A courtyard or patio is an outdoor space that is contained by walls. This provides a sense of security and enclosure and is a crucial element of a traditional design, providing privacy and an intimate ambience. It also serves as the atmospheric backdrop to the stage set of your garden, giving it a unique character.

Above: *This old flint and red brick wall is complemented by the apricot climbing rose.*

A Choice of Old or New

An old brick wall will immediately confer a sense of presence. City houses from the 18th and 19th centuries frequently feature such walls and they are also found in developments formed from large country estates. If your home is situated adjacent to an early industrial or institutional building, you might be lucky enough to have a high flank wall forming part of your boundary. If you have any existing walls, you have an ideal starting point for your patio design. If the condition of the brickwork is poor, it would be worth paying to have the joints repointed.

Many old walls have had patching-up repairs, often carried out with non-matching bricks. While it is a shame to paint brickwork, it may be a cleaner solution, using a pale tone that will help to reflect light.

Above: *A niche in this stone wall is supported by small stone pilasters.*

If they don't exist, consider building new walls. While not cheap, brick is traditional and would be the best option if it matches the house style. Reclaimed brick can usually be found for this purpose, and new,

handmade bricks are also available. Alternatively, walls can be built from cement blockwork, cheaper to buy and easier to construct. However, this is not pretty and the blockwork needs to be cement rendered, which can be pre-tinted or painted. This gives you a clean, bright background.

Plants for Walls

Climbing plants are an essential component of a traditional walled garden, transforming a blank façade into a lively and voluptuous tableau of flowers and foliage. A built wall gives the perfect support for fully grown specimens, which can be heavy and vulnerable to the effects of winds and storms. Climbers need a strong supporting structure, and walls are far more appropriate for this than fences, which are liable to movement.

Climbing plants cling by different means. Some, such as Virginia creeper *(Parthenocissus quinquefolia)* and common ivy *(Hedera helix)*, need no extra help as they attach themselves by means of suckers or adventitious roots. Others need a helping hand: passion flowers attach themselves with tendrils, while clematis twine their leaf stems around supports. Trellis works for a lightweight clematis (see opposite for planting clematis), but most need something stronger. You can fix a series of robust steel wires, spaced horizontally 30–40cm (12–18in) apart, to the wall using bolts and

Left: *A red brick screen wall divides up the garden to create a courtyard space, with an elegant arched doorway inviting passage.*

tensioning devices. Virtually invisible, this can hold up the heaviest of climbing species.

Climbers are always trying to reach impossible heights and mix with their neighbours, so in a restrained set-up you might need to formalize the display. Some species lend themselves to 'vertical pruning' by training the stems over wire forms fixed to the wall. Simple geometric shapes are easiest, but will need to be trimmed in spring and autumn. Evergreen climbers are a rarity, but the star jasmine (*Trachelospermum jasminoides*), with its dark foliage and perfumed white flowers, is perfect for a formal scheme. On a high wall with plenty of space, *Vitis coignetiae* can be trained in a similar way. This ambitious vine drops its huge leaves in winter, but not before unleashing glorious autumn tints of fiery vermilion.

PLANTING CLEMATIS AGAINST TRELLIS

In a traditional patio, classic flowering climbers such as clematis and roses help to set the scene, especially when they are combined with trellis. The summer- and autumn-flowering *Clematis viticella* shown here is ideal for small courtyards because in early spring you need to cut them back to about 30cm (12in) from ground level.

1 Select the position for the trellis and drill holes for the battens. Use plastic wall plugs and the appropriate size of screws. Screw the battens to the wall and fix your stained or painted trellis to the battens using galvanized nails or screws.

2 Fork over the planting area, removing any perennial weeds and working in organic matter such as home-made garden compost (soil mix). This ensures that the ground has sufficient moisture-holding capacity to support the plant.

3 Water the plant before removing from its pot. Dig a hole 30cm (1ft) away from the wall and twice the width and depth of the pot. Mix in a scattering of bonemeal, using latex gloves. Bury 10cm (4in) of the stem to encourage shooting. Backfill and water.

4 Climbers often come tightly fastened to a single cane and it helps to undo and separate the individual stems and fix them on to the trellis, bringing them close to the horizontal to stimulate flower and side shoot production. Use climber ties or soft twine.

Above: *This elaborate design shows a curved feature alcove covered with treillage, which tricks the eye into a false perspective.*

Left: *A combination of square and diamond mesh trellis panels, fixed in a timber framework, creates a garden backdrop, discreetly obscuring the terrace behind.*

Classical Treillage

French-style trellis, or treillage, is a traditional material, which creates an instant classical effect to decorate the blank walls of enclosed courtyards. It evokes a *trompe l'oeil* illusion by arranging a series of two-dimensional panels along the wall. Combinations of curved shapes and tall rectangles trick the eye into seeing three-dimensional walls and archways, thus increasing the impression of space and dimension. Climbing plants that would obscure the effect are not used here but mirrors might be introduced to increase the illusion.

Shaped treillage is available in many qualities and can be purchased ready-made, or you can commission a design. The panels are made up of narrow timber slats interwoven in diamond and square patterns, resulting in a silhouette of shapes that stand out against the supporting wall. The effect is best achieved by painting the treillage a colour that contrasts with a plain background. Period colours generally work best, offering an elegant solution when creating a restrained patio design.

The device is a brilliant way to clothe the walls of a courtyard. The rhythm of movement it provides is an especially successful technique to open up other potentially claustrophobic environments, such as a narrow entrance way, or to diminish the pace of a long wall.

By including panels of mirror in the design, the illusion of space can be further enhanced. This works particularly well when the mirrored panels are incorporated into arched sections of treillage. In the same way as mirrors in an interior, the reflected background appears to become a secondary area into which to pass, thus doubling the impression of size. The additional bonus is that reflected light will enhance what is often, by default, a shady area.

Trellis Screens

The enclosure theme can be developed by means of trellis screens to divide up the courtyard space into 'rooms', which add dimension to the garden and serve as secret places. This device is an effective and sophisticated way to create the surrounding boundaries for a roof garden space. The screens can conceal a quiet seating spot, hide a surprise feature such as a fountain, or simply disguise a service area. The individual screening panels might be formed from a criss-cross of fine diagonal slats that result in a high level of privacy while still admitting light. Curved archways, clothed in climbers, can be used to provide access to individual areas and to open up specific spaces, while long planting boxes incorporated between the screens will add interest to the design. This is an effective way of planting in a roof garden with solid floors.

Ready-made trellis panels enable you to make up your specific design, and include shaped profiles offering curved tops, arches, and panels with openings to allow a view through to what lies beyond. Differing formats of weaving the slats include diagonal lines and diamond patterns in a range of spacings and sizes. With such a wide range of options available it is possible to create a variety of patio effects. However, when budgets are tight, trellis at its simplest can be purchased ready to take away in rectangular panels of various sizes from garden centres and home-improvement stores.

Fencing Panels

It may be necessary to create or replace a boundary enclosure. The cheapest and most easily installed option is to use ready-made timber fencing panels, fixed a little above ground level to wooden posts set in concrete footings. Use solid portions where you need to provide privacy, then relieve the monotony by interspersing trellis screens over which you can train attractive climbing plants. Basic trellis offers an economic way to increase the height of an existing boundary wall or fence, its lightweight construction making it easy to fix by means of timber battens and bolts.

In most locations the maximum height restriction between gardens is 1.8m (6ft). You can fix narrow trellis panels to the top of the solid sections to give a higher screening effect without normally contravening building regulations, but check with your local authority. Discuss your proposals with neighbours before starting any boundary work.

Hedges

Topiary-like evergreen hedges have a role as a stabilizing element of green architecture and can be good partition substitutes in the formal, traditional garden – and these are much less expensive than stone or brick. Low-hedging materials include the upright form of rosemary, compact lavenders, *Santolina* (cotton lavender) and *Euonymus*. To achieve a crisp-edged effect use dwarf and ordinary box, golden or plain yew. These varieties cut surprisingly well as a low but wide block of a hedge. Or for a speedy, economical option try *Lonicera nitida*, the small-leaved evergreen honeysuckle with an ideal growth for hedging.

Below: *This arched trellis feature decorates the painted brick wall, making an excellent framing device for the tall, planted vase.*

Below: *A low hedge is used here to define the perimeters of a courtyard space that has more extensive grounds beyond.*

PLANTS AND CONTAINERS FOR TRADITIONAL SPACES

The design and material of containers for planting will exert a strong influence on your garden, and will help to reinforce the traditional theme. Equally important is to combine containers with complementary planting. It is a question of shape and proportion, and the intrinsic characteristics of pot and plant.

Above: *A collection of annuals, with a central cordyline, growing in a container.*

Classical Shapes

Italianate-style terracotta pots make a handsome contribution to a classical garden design. Their generous proportions and warm colour introduce a timeless stateliness and an image of shady terraced gardens under an azure sky. The 'lemon pot' style, with a wide mouth, narrowing gently to the base, is a perfect container for clipped box topiary, complementing the form of a round ball shape or a taller pyramid. Its restrained, dark green foliage would make a year-round evergreen sculptural statement. A vase-shaped container, supported on a stem, lends itself to floral displays, such as deep blue agapanthus to suggest a Tuscan heritage, or seasonally changing colour, such as hyacinths, for spring or cascades of deepest red, ivy-leaf geraniums for an elegant summer display.

Traditional Materials

Terracotta is a natural and practical material for planting containers because, being porous, it enables the soil to dry out evenly all over its surface. This results in slow evaporation, which, in turn, facilitates a good balance of water and air in the soil mix. If your region suffers regularly from winter temperatures below 0°C (32°F), you should choose

Left: *This classical stone vase and plinth are balanced perfectly by the soft planting of trailing helichrysum.*

Below: *Blue hyacinths and muscari set off the colour and form of this terracotta vase.*

only frost-proof pots. These will have been kiln fired at a minimum temperature of 1,000°C (1,832°F).

Handmade terracotta pots stand out dramatically from machine-made ones. If money is no object, then select magnificent examples from Impruneta near Florence, in Italy, fine enough to be passed down the generations as family treasures. However, there are also excellent-quality frost-proof pots made in the UK, and convincing replicas of more expensive pots made in China.

Replica Containers

Reproductions of classical stone urns are an alternative choice, especially if your local building materials are of stone. They can be found in different tones through whitish/grey and soft beige/yellow to complement the garden surroundings, while a buff pink can work well with red brick. These containers are formed in moulds

Above: *Red zonal geraniums partner a rope-edged, terracotta pot in a wall niche.*

and made from reconstituted stone – ground-up stone offcuts blended with cement to hold the shape. These are robust and handsome, especially when combined with raised detailing. The bright, new finish can be induced to weather down to a patina by applying a

Above: *Terracotta is ideal for plant pots, staying relatively cool in hot weather.*

proprietary aging product or by brushing them with natural (plain) yogurt. Because their characteristics echo traditional styles, evergreen topiary planting subjects, such as box, bay and holly, are suitably bold in form and structure to reflect the bulk of the container.

PLANTING A BAY TREE

The sweetly aromatic foliage of the bay tree has been a feature of formal Mediterranean gardens since antiquity. These are somewhat tender, and planting them in pots allows you to move them to a more sheltered spot over winter. Pot on specimens as they grow and at the same time begin training to a simple geometric shape such as a ball or cone. Or train with a single stem to create a standard or lollipop.

1 Choose a large pot with an inside diameter of at least 38cm (15in), except for small specimens that are to be grown on. Select clay or ceramic pots that won't blow over and add pieces of broken clay pots or pour in large-size gravel to cover drainage holes.

2 Part-fill with a loam-based compost (soil mix). Soak the bay tree in its container in a bucket of water, then knock the plant out. If wiry roots are tightly wound around the root ball, gently tease out a few. Test the plant for size and position.

3 Add or remove soil as necessary so that the top of the root-ball (roots) and soil level will be 2.5–5cm (1–2in) below the pot rim. Firm the compost around the roots, as evergreen trees like bay offer a great deal of wind resistance. Water thoroughly.

4 Add pot feet to keep the pot off the ground and maintain good drainage. Trim to shape with secateurs (pruners), avoiding cutting leaves in half as this causes brown edges. Shape between late spring and late summer to avoid new shoots becoming frosted.

Above: *A spiky* Agave americana *adds extra texture to this interesting low wall.*

Left: *A sequence of classical faux-lead containers, reinforced by tall, clipped* Ligustrum jonandrum, *border this canal.*

Planting to Fit

The built elements of a patio form a clean, unchanging backdrop for the planting scheme. Together they should create a harmonious balance, with the hard materials playing a strong supporting role to set off the energy of the plants. A plant's personality is expressed through its habit, shape, texture and leaf form. With many thousands of plants from which to choose, identify their individual characters and select those that fit into the planting theme.

Evergreens are the solid citizens, slow growing and important for the creation of a framework. They play a valuable role in the traditional style when clipped into tight shapes, and work well when arranged in formal lines or groups. Large boxwood balls and pyramids are especially handsome, while bay looks impressive grown as a standard on a tall, bare stem. Holly also lends itself to this treatment, looking more curvaceously chunky and appealing than its looser bush form.

Choosing Traditional Pots

Many traditional containers, such as those made of stone and terracotta, are very heavy. However, if you don't intend to move them once they are in place then there is no reason to deliberately avoid them – indeed their very weight gives substance and focus. Also featuring among the planter heavyweights is cast lead. They are usually replicas of Elizabethan or Regency pieces, and these finely detailed designs with their classical elegance belie their massive loading. But unless you cannot live without a dramatic lead cistern filled with ravishing black Queen of Night tulips, perhaps you would do best to restrain your selection to smaller rectangular forms.

In most circumstances, good-quality faux-lead reproductions made from glass fibre and resin are perfectly acceptable. These are quite convincing and are particularly useful where weight loading is an issue, such as on a roof terrace or balcony.

The best square-shaped planters for a traditional scheme are based on those conceived for the citrus and palm trees at Versailles, outside Paris, that make their annual transition from the huge orangery to the immense terraces. Taking the name of the palace, the 'Versailles tub' has become a perennial favourite. Normally made of timber, they are sometimes banded with steel, as the originals were designed to be taken apart. They are available in sizes able to accommodate a small tree.

Right: *Hosta is an essential foliage perennial for shady pots and ground cover. H. 'Blue Cadet' has striking mauve blooms.*

Far right: *Hebe in a classic-shaped pot, with simple stripes mirroring the flower colour.*

Spiky leafed individuals, such as yuccas and dracaenas, are the outgoing party-lovers of the world, making strong contrast statements, and they look especially good in a bold container. Small-leaved, mound-forming reclusives, such as *Hebe pinguifolia*, with its tiny glaucous leaves, are good for cushioning bed edges, while feathery cotton lavender (*Santolina chamaecyparissus*) can be arranged into architectural groups of clipped grey-green spheres.

A clothing of energetic climbers is an essential backdrop. *Clematis armandii* and *Trachelospermum* *jasminoides* offer an evergreen screen with scented white flowers in spring and summer, respectively. Perennials are the showmen, bursting from the earth in spring to create a wealth of forms and textures. For style and elegance, nothing beats the hosta's veined foliage, combining sumptuous tones of grey, sulphur and lime.

CLIPPING A SPIRAL

Unlike symmetrical shapes, spirals brim with energy and movement. These classic topiary shapes look impressive and upmarket, and are relatively simple to create. Use the training technique below, but keep in mind the eventual size required. Either start with a bigger cone or add to the initial number of coils over time, merging lower coils and reshaping. When it is complete, avoid standing the spiral hard up against a wall, where one side could be heavily shaded, and turn it regularly. To make this easier, fix castors or stand the pot on a wheeled plinth.

1 Start with a cone with a single central stem that has been clipped several times to create dense interior growth. Tie string or raffia to the top of the plant, or start at the base, and wind it around as shown.

2 Using a pair of secateurs (pruning shears) or small hand shears, cut the initial groove. Go gently at first, working from the top of the plant down. Carefully cut any larger branches with secateurs. Keep standing back to survey progress.

3 Deepen the groove and create a coil with a rounded profile, rather like a snail shell. Stand the plant out of strong sun and wind, water regularly and feed with dilute liquid fertilizer. Clip in late spring and late summer to maintain its shape.

STRUCTURES AND FURNITURE FOR TRADITIONAL SPACES

To make the most of the available space, the vertical dimension in a patio must be utilized. Pergolas, arbours and gazebos, all traditional garden elements, provide decorative, three-dimensional forms that introduce focal points and ways to create separate areas. Timber or metal garden furniture provides the finishing touch.

Above: *A flowering yellow laburnum climbing over a pergola structure.*

Pergolas

A pergola is a freestanding structure formed from vertical wooden posts or stone pillars, which support rails that cross over the top to carry climbing plants. A versatile device, it has been used in gardens for centuries. The Romans liked to create shaded paths with overhead cover, while early illustrated manuscripts show latticed structures being used to support grapevines in medieval courtyards.

In a traditional garden, you might use a rose arch to frame the entrance to a long, romantic walkway displaying trailing wisteria. A pergola can also be adapted to become an arbour to make a cosy dining or seating place along a wall. In this

case, support posts are required only along the outside edge, while the rails are extended and fixed securely to the supporting wall by means of metal brackets. The flexibility of this type of construction means that it can be incorporated into any size of patio.

Pergolas can be constructed entirely from timber, which suits a 19th-century or Arts and Crafts style. The supporting posts should be made from bold, heavy sections, oak being a suitable choice. The cross rails can be somewhat lighter, but still sturdy (see construction method on page 95). Simple, economic wooden structures can be bought off the shelf, and posts might be clothed with trellis panels to disguise them. A pale, period-effect, painted or stained finish instantly upgrades an off-the-peg pergola.

Above: *This bold but simple gazebo makes a compelling focal point, framing a paved court and magnificent planting.*

Gazebos and Obelisks

The gazebo is a kind of garden folly that makes a fabulous focal point and a glorious dining area. Romantic styles work well for a traditional plot, especially when constructed from forged metal or, for an even lighter effect, delicate 19th-century-style wirework. Perfumed rambling roses, jasmine and honeysuckle would all make perfect planting subjects to enhance enhance warm summer days.

When a gazebo is made more weatherproof, protected with timber side panels and a solid roof finished with tiles, slates or metal such as copper or zinc, it has a wider range of uses.

Above: *A delightfully romantic, tiled roof folly makes the perfect, shady trysting spot.*

Where space is tight, or to add to the vertical texture of a larger patio space, you can use obelisks to introduce height. Place singly to create focal points or arrange in formal groupings – to set the corners of a parterre for example, or in rows. A pair of classically proportioned timber obelisks would handsomely frame an entrance door or mark the start of a formal pathway. Placed in a timber Versailles planter, an obelisk would make a fitting, stand-alone feature, best planted with an evergreen, such as the star jasmine (*Trachelospermum jasminoides*) or one of the smaller-leaved ivies. For a romantic garden theme, a more delicate steel or wirework obelisk would marry well with a large-flowered clematis or a pillar rose.

Right: *These tall, timber obelisks provide an excellent vehicle for climbing* Mina lobata *and completely alter the scale and presence of the parterre.*

BUILDING A TRELLIS ARBOUR

Decorative trellis panels, including shaped pieces, are available in a wide range of sizes. With some basic practical skills, you should be able to fit these to a framework of posts to create your own traditional garden arbour. You can also incorporate solid timber to form a seat, or you can place a bench under the canopy. Cover the arbour with climbers, such as honeysuckle and jasmine, to scent the air and provide leafy seclusion.

1 Trim the wooden posts to 2m (6ft), not forgetting to add the depth of the metal 'shoe' at the top of the spike that holds them in the ground. Check that you have all the trellis components, including the 2m x 90cm (6 x 3ft) back panel.

2 Set the posts for the back panel 2m (6ft) apart and use a club hammer to drive in the spiked metal post supports. With a No 8 drill bit, drill holes for the galvanized screws at intervals down each side of the trellis, then screw the panel into position.

3 Repeat this method to fix first the side panels – each 2m x 60cm (6 x 2ft) – then the narrow front panels and, as a decorative addition above, the shaped trellis section. Finally fit the 2m x 60cm (6 x 2ft) roof panel.

4 Paint the arbour with an exterior-quality wood stain. On ground too hard or stony to drive in post fixing spikes, use longer posts and dig holes to accommodate post bases and quick-setting, ready-mix concrete.

Above: *The climbers on this gazebo are supported with a central tree-trunk pillar and a metal-framed circular structure.*

Above: *Reclaimed cast-iron columns provide a strong and elegant support for this timber-roofed pergola.*

Appropriate Materials

Patios with a neoclassical theme demand elegantly proportioned columns to support the overhead structure. It is worth searching reclamation yards for suitable timber and stone beams that can be adapted to suit your purpose. Alternatively, use reproductions in reconstituted stone, sturdy timber uprights, or brick columns, if this fits with the style of the surrounding architecture. With the help of a builder or carpenter, a substantial design incorporating steel or timber for top rails can easily be created. This style requires planting of appropriate grandeur, and wisteria, with its pendant racemes or frothy rambler roses, seems best able to rise to the occasion.

Where the appearance of visual lightness is required, forged steel is an excellent material. Its combination of inherent physical strength and total flexibility allows it to be formed into fine and complex designs such as a period-style gazebo or rose bower. A wide range of structures can be purchased direct, or a blacksmith could create a composition dovetailed to your design.

Climbing plants can become exceedingly heavy, and the physical exposure of vertical structures makes them susceptible to wind pressure and the extra weight of snow. The main considerations when building pergolas, arbours or gazebos, therefore, is that they should be well constructed from stout materials, and that the vertical supports should be bedded firmly into the ground with concrete foundations.

Right: *This colonnaded arbour with cream pillars supporting a wooden frame looks toward a stunning sea view.*

Timber Furniture

The most traditional and robust designs of furniture tend to be made from timber. Seating forms are generous and shapes vary from rectangular and solid towards the more curvaceous lines of the rolled-arm bench, known as 'Lutyens-style', and lounging steamer chairs.

Most are made from exotic hardwoods, of which teak is the most beautiful and luxurious. These woods are weatherproof and need little upkeep, however, do ensure that your products are sourced sustainably. Oak is a handsome alternative, but should be properly seasoned to prevent it leaching tannin, which can stain paving. The best timbers can be left untreated, and over time they acquire a wonderful, silvery patina. If you prefer a more finished look, use a quality yacht varnish or give the wood an annual application of purpose-made oil. If you prefer a painted look, to make a focal point or to complement another feature, choose softwood, which does not contain resins that can resist the finish.

Right: *Filigree, cast-aluminium furniture mimics the Victorian style, but is lighter in weight than the original cast-iron versions.*

Above: *This untreated teak bench takes on a silvery patina, setting off perfectly the red and orange dahlias and nasturtiums.*

Metal Furniture

Lightweight wirework chairs and tables make a charming addition to a metal gazebo, reflecting the delicate tracery of the design, or would integrate subtly into a secluded corner. A Regency-style forged-steel bench makes a

Above: *Curvaceous, American Adirondack-style seats from the early 20th century are becoming a new garden design classic.*

handsome, understated feature, while chairs of a similar style can be combined with a metal dining or occasional table. Check that metal furniture is rust proofed before leaving it outside in all weathers. All metal can be painted, helping to keep it in good repair.

ORNAMENT FOR TRADITIONAL SPACES

Traditional statuary and ornament should be chosen to suggest a period style and to harmonize with surrounding architecture and materials. Placed in a key position, a classical statue creates a focal point, and can be lit at night for further emphasis. Decorative finials can also be used to embellish pillars and balustrades.

Above: *This stone ball finial gives the finishing touch to a carved stone balustrade.*

Sculptural Options

Introducing figurative form may seem to be the most natural direction to take in a garden setting, and animal and human forms have a familiarity in a traditional garden. Certainly, reproductions of classical figures are an understandably popular choice and allow you to emulate the glories of earlier centuries in your patio design. To make a strong, single statement, a Greek goddess, or perhaps philosopher, set against a hedge of dark, clipped topiary would add an appropriate air of calm and order. You can also integrate animals very well – a reclining lion gazing down from a terrace could look very handsome, while a jousting unicorn or tusked wild boar could add a more fantastical touch to a formal pool. Mythical sea creatures and leonine masks work extremely well as spouts for wall fountains.

By contrast, geometrically architectural pieces are pure and unemotional. Obelisks provide punctuation points to mark an entrance or pathway, while you can use columns, crumbling or otherwise, to form circles and lines, or set them singly among a group of plants. Smaller pieces, known as finials, shaped as balls, acorns and pineapples, make excellent finishing touches for gateposts. Make your own by scattering bits of reclaimed or salvaged stonework on the ground, like the remains of an ancient ruin.

Tall, classical vases, often standing on plinths, play an important role as ornament and are useful vehicles by which to introduce seasonal bedding. Generally, the planting space is small, so they are best when dressed with elegant flowers, such as tulips and trailing geraniums, with sophisticated colours of pure white and deepest wine red to suit. Wider, freestanding urns are best balanced by clipped box or other topiary plants.

Style and Materials

Hand-carved stone sculpture would be a fabulous and luxurious addition to a traditional garden, as would cast bronze, which is perennially popular for use outside. Antiques are costly, however, but all types of reproductions are widely available, using fibreglass and bronze substitutes. These do vary enormously in quality and finish, so do some research before ordering.

The style of the piece will dictate the material, but reconstituted stone is a popular choice. Its new appearance can be easily 'distressed' by the application of a proprietary treatment, or see the paint treatment opposite. Alternatively, if placed in a damp and shady spot, it will not take long for algae and moss to appear. Most designs can be found in this material.

As an alternative to the cool, pale colour of stone, choose the warmer tones of terracotta. Urns and vases should be made from frost-resistant materials. Cast-iron reproductions are an inexpensive choice, with lead as the luxurious option. Quality, handmade terracotta is handsome, while stone dust and cement mixes offer attractive-looking alternatives.

Above: *A classical figure, moulded from reconstituted stone, resin and concrete.*

Above: *This cast-iron vase has had a wash of white paint to relieve the intentional rust.*

HOW TO AGE NEW STONEWARE

Carved stone ornaments are expensive and reconstituted stone pieces are not cheap. For a more economical option, look for concrete ornaments that have been moulded from originals. These ornaments will eventually weather and age and become colonized with algae, but, if you want an instant transformation, follow the technique below and achieve the same effect in just a couple of hours.

1 Use a solution of PVA glue, diluted according to the manufacturer's instructions, to seal the concrete surface, including the inside. Repeat as necessary, and allow it to dry. This will prevent moisture from penetrating the concrete and lifting the paint layers.

2 Paint the ornament with a base coat of white emulsion, then, once it is dry, follow with a roughly applied coat of pale grey. This can be mixed by adding a touch of black artist's acrylic paint. The vase now has the appearance of newly carved stone.

3 Use a piece of dampened natural sponge to stipple on darker areas of grey and charcoal acrylic paint, working it into the cracks and crevices to accentuate the relief design and emphasize shadows. The vase is beginning to look more weathered.

4 If possible, find a photograph of mosses and algae colonizing stone to give you a colour and texture reference to work from. Mix up a palette of artist's acrylics in greens and yellows to mimic the plants and apply the colours randomly with the sponge.

5 Once you have achieved a natural-looking covering, with some darker green areas under the bowl and around the base and lighter yellowish greens on any prominent features, such as the fruits and swags here, brush on random patches of bright ochre to mimic lichen colonies.

6 Allow the paint to dry between each coat, then weatherproof the mock-aged patina by sealing it with a couple of coats of clear, matt exterior varnish. Set the vase on top of a plinth or wall column, cementing the base for added safety.

WATER FEATURES FOR TRADITIONAL SPACES

Water introduces a unique dimension of reflection and sound and features often have an architectural contribution. A built feature with formal lines and structure is the most appropriate for a traditional scheme. A water feature in this style will be defined by its ornamental impact, and by the nature of the water flow.

Above: *The sight and sound of a splashing fountain brings life and light to the garden.*

Using Pools

An above-ground pool makes a strong architectural statement and a striking focal point. It can be constructed from low walls, around 50–60cm (20–24in) high, using brick or natural stone. You can also use economical concrete blocks faced up in stone slips or rendered in stucco. A wider seating ledge, perhaps of smooth, dark slate instead of a simple coping, would encourage people to sit and enjoy the feature close up. A round shape is usually thought to be the most attractive, but a rectangular form is easier to build – important if you are doing it yourself.

A water feature at ground level can be a garden highlight, especially if it is set within an area of paving. Where space allows, two or more pools can be linked by a narrow channel, or rill, bordered on each side by a flagstone path. This creates a directional effect, leading the eye towards a garden feature, such as a statue or vase.

MAKING A CONCRETE POOL

Concrete pools are suitable in places where soil conditions are too unstable for sunken pools with flexible liners. They are also good for raised pools, which need strong sides to withstand water pressure.

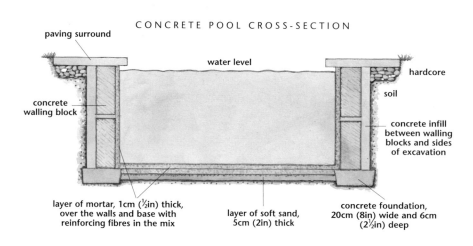

CONCRETE POOL CROSS-SECTION

paving surround
water level
hardcore
soil
concrete walling block
concrete infill between walling blocks and sides of excavation
layer of mortar, 1cm (½in) thick, over the walls and base with reinforcing fibres in the mix
layer of soft sand, 5cm (2in) thick
concrete foundation, 20cm (8in) wide and 6cm (2½in) deep

1 Mark out the outline of the pool with string and canes. Dig out the area to a depth of 75cm (30in). If you are keeping the soil, do not mix topsoil and subsoil.
2 Dig a 20cm- (8in-) wide trench to a depth of 6cm (2½in) around the inside of the base. Add the concrete and level the top. Check with a spirit level. Leave to dry.
3 Dig out about 6cm (2½in) soil from the base. Spread and rake, removing stones, then level and firm a 5cm (2in) layer of soft sand below the top of the foundation.

4 Skim the sand with a 1cm (½in) layer of fibre-reinforced mortar with a plasterer's trowel, overlapping the concrete foundations by 5cm (2in).
5 After 24 hours, mortar concrete walling blocks on to the foundations and check the levels. Once set, fill in the gap between the soil wall and the walling blocks with a stiff concrete mix. Fill in the inside of the blocks if they have cavities.
6 Allow a further 48 hours for the whole structure to set thoroughly. Dampen the

whole surface of the internal structure before covering with a 1cm (½in) layer of fibre-reinforced mortar. To give added strength, make a rounded cornice edge where the walls meet each other and the base.
7 Replace the top 10cm (4in) of soil with hardcore. Mortar the paving edge on to the pool walls and the hardcore base. Place the paving surround so that it overlaps the inside wall by 2.5–5cm (1–2in).
8 Allow the internal walls to dry, then paint with a black waterproof sealant.

Fountains

Ornamental fountains in traditional gardens animate the more formal static elements of structure and planting. You can direct a fountain water jet through a sculptural ornament secured to the base of the pool, or it can spray directly from below the water's surface.

Installing Water Features

Water animates a space and in a smaller area will provide a central focus. A functional water feature involves watertight construction, electrics, as well as pumps and filters.

To stay clean, water needs to recirculate, and using a fountain powered by a submersible pump is a practical method to achieve this.

A rill would have to be excavated, lined and waterproofed, but the depth of water can be shallow. For the best results, a very dark lining imparts a sombre tone to the water and maximizes reflectivity. A separate water aeration and filtering pump would be needed.

You can create a wall fountain using a water-filled trough, fed by a spout in the wall above. Use an old

Above: *The black liner of this raised pool is a sober backdrop against the stone facings.*

stone or reproduction trough and combine the spout with a figurative mask with the mouth as the spout. The electrics and recirculating pump mechanism can be concealed behind the wall, or a small immersion pump disguised below the water's surface.

An underwater luminaire will provide the finishing touch for a night-time display.

Above: *The pump mechanism for this fountain unit is hidden behind the wall.*

Safety notes: *Take precautions to prevent children having access to ponds and other water features. Use a fence to deter toddlers from ponds and pools.*

Wherever electricity and water are used together, use an electrician to carry out the work.

Above: *A tiny feature can make a big impact; the pump is disguised below a shelf of cobbles in this self-contained unit.*

Above: *Built from stone slabs, this above-ground pool includes a seating ledge to enjoy the fountain at close hand.*

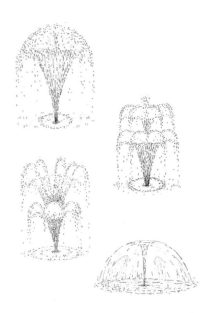

Above: *Submersible pumps come with a range of attachments to produce most of the more common small fountain shapes.*

LIGHTING FOR TRADITIONAL SPACES

The lighting in a traditional patio is subtle. Low-level path lighting and period-style wall lights enable the garden to be enjoyed at night with a degree of safety, and spot lights may also be used to create one or two dramatic statements, enlivening views from inside the house at night as well as outdoors.

Above: *Solar garden lights are ideal for lining a walkway or garden path.*

Wall Lights

Whatever period in history you take as your inspiration, when selecting wall lamps it is important to choose models that are in proportion with the space and to pick a style that blends with existing garden furniture, containers and ornamental features. Remember these lights will be very much on show and will add to the overall design theme of the garden.

There are scores of different models for wall lights but for period settings, Victorian-style coach lamps in black, white or weathered metallic finishes are popular and mimic the wrought-iron and cast-iron designs of old. Some of these designs are solid and chunky and work best against a backdrop of stone or rendered walls and within simply dressed, more functional spaces. For this type of setting and in more rustic locations also consider brass bulkhead lights.

Creating a Co-ordinated Look

You can often buy matching lamp-posts to go with wall lights, as well as lamps to fit on the top of gateposts. Ask to see supplier catalogues for the full range.

A softer look comes in the form of Art Nouveau inspired lights with a simple ball-shaped globe supported by an ornate arm or scrolled support. Italianate or Venetian-style wall lanterns are also available, sometimes in an attractive verdigris finish. These may be modelled on original lanterns and will certainly add to the charm of the patio.

Path and Step Lighting

There are two options for lighting pathways. One is to choose period-style lanterns on short posts to use in a line along path edges and seating areas. Another much less conspicuous approach is to use small white floor lights that fit in flush with paving. The black or brushed-steel surround is hardly noticeable. Alternatively, use modern black spots along the edge of paths and angle the lamp to shine down and across the stone, brickwork or gravel. Plants will hide the wires and fittings. Concentrate lighting particularly where there are steps and changes in level or direction. On a still summer's evening, you can use nightlights or small candles up either side of a flight of steps or along the top of a retaining wall to highlight the symmetry and formality of your patio.

Above: *The curling metal embellishments on this lantern add to its romantic appeal.*

Outdoor Dining

Oil or candle lanterns radiate the warm glow of a natural flame and create the nostalgic feeling of a time before electric lights. Outdoor candelabras are an inspiring sight when lit at night and they can also provide interesting decorative detail during the day. Choose from suspended candelabras that are supported on a chain used for raising and lowering, table candelabras and floor candelabras.

Traditional oil lamps, including brass lanterns, give out a soft glow and are an effective lighting option for night-time get-togethers. Never leave naked flames unattended.

Highlighting Elements

By day the garden is a constantly changing scene of sunshine and shadow and the form and texture

Above: *This functional lamp set against brickwork fits a Victorian courtyard theme.*

of sculptural elements becomes prominent only when shadows are sharply defined. But as the night draws in you have the opportunity to be much more theatrical, maximizing the contours of carved stonework, sculpture and even topiary using carefully positioned mini spots, either mains-voltage or solar-powered.

Always experiment first before setting the lights into their final positions. A powerful torch is a useful aid. You can light from either side, from the front and at points in between or try backlighting for carved screens. Wall masks and classical busts can look dramatic when the lights is directed just below the chin. In darkness, you can select just a few pieces for lighting and if these elements were ones largely hidden during the daytime, you could achieve a completely different feel when the lighting comes on at night. Subtly highlight raised beds, formal clipped hedges or pillars using uplighters, spots or mini floodlights.

Lighting Water Features

A simple idea for a summer party is to set night-lights at regular intervals around the edge of a raised or sunken pool. Still water can also look magical when lit from below using specialist lamps. But rather than simply lighting up the whole pool, it can be more impressive if you simply spotlight a water cascade from below or shine light up on to a water sculpture. Some fountain arrangements have integral lighting. As with any outdoor water feature, always employ a qualified electrician to ensure that the system is safely installed.

Right: *The framework of this traditional pergola is softly illuminated by several hidden spotlights.*

Above: *This limestone-lined canal flanked by pleached lime draws the eye to the Venetian-style well head at the end. As the light fades, the carved stonework becomes an even more dramatic focal point, lit by underwater spots set between the stepping-stones. These act as camouflage for the lights during the day.*

MEDITERRANEAN WARMTH

The Mediterranean patio or courtyard is a sensuous place. On summer evenings, protected from the elements by sheltering, climber-clad walls, the atmosphere is warm and heavy with exotic fragrance. Candle lanterns flicker enchantingly. This is the perfect place for unwinding after work or sharing a glass of wine with friends. If rain threatens, a chiminea-heated loggia provides a comfortable retreat.

During the day, the vibrant colour and texture of flower-filled pots and raised beds is a feast for the eye. Terracotta and ochre shades mingle with sky and cornflower blues of doors and shutters.

The taste of food magnifies when eaten alfresco under the dappled shade of a tree or vine-covered pergola, and the scent of aromatic oils released from herbs and scented shrubs intensifies with the trapped heat and humidity. Close your eyes and soothe your senses by listening to the hum of bees on lavender and the sound of gently trickling water.

Left: *This sunlit corner features some of the typical elements of the Mediterranean style, including an old stone wall as a rustic backdrop and a jumble of pots with bright flowers.*

FLOORING FOR MEDITERRANEAN SPACES

With a legacy of classical Greek and Roman architecture and later Moorish influences, Mediterranean gardens have often featured beautifully crafted floors of mosaics, tiles, cobbles and setts. You can adapt tradition and add contemporary decorative flourishes utilizing the many different materials available today.

Above: *Herbs and alpines nestle between rugged stepping stones and pebbles.*

Simple Solutions

In small and unusually shaped courtyards, a plain flooring solution can help to throw the focus on to the plants and other decorative elements. Various grades of gravel, especially natural-looking pebble and shingle mixtures, work better than crushed stone, though rolled and compacted clay aggregate offers an excellent alternative. Choose warm-coloured materials, such as golden gravel or toffee-coloured flint, to create the illusion of a sunnier climate. To avoid weeds, cover the soil with landscape fabric first. Avoid fine-graded gravel, which tends to be kicked about.

Textural Choices

Try contrasting gravel with square or rectangular paving or exterior-quality ceramic tiles. Square and rectangular elements are best laid out so that the sides of adjacent pieces

Above: *Reclaimed timber planks create a pathway across a loose surface of pebbles.*

are parallel. For example, a widely spaced grid pattern could be used or a staggered line forming a relaxed path. You can be more informal with randomly shaped stone. Weathered reclaimed timbers may also be sunk in flush with the ground surface to create a wide meandering walkway or to mark a seating area.

Another option is to create a graded beach effect by working larger cobbles and pebbles into corners and against walls. Buy bags of pebbles in different sizes whose colours and textures combine well. Use the smaller grades at the front to blend in with the gravel and bring a few of the larger cobbles and rounded boulders forwards.

Concrete is frequently used to surface gardens in hot climates and it is an inexpensive alternative to paving if you want a smooth, solid surface. However, concrete alone looks too stark in a Mediterranean-

Above: *Differently coloured gravel, pebbles and cobbles can be used to create informal patterns that flow into the borders.*

style garden unless you lay it in smaller panels bordered by, for example, natural stone setts. You can soften the look of concrete by working shingle, pebbles and even quantities of cockleshells (available bagged) into the top layer. To create a weathered effect, brush away some of the cement with a stiff nylon hand brush dipped in a bucket of water before the mix sets to expose more of the pebbles.

A Cobbled Yard

For a more obvious pebble or cobble surface, lay mortar over compacted hardcore and press larger cobbles or pebbles into the surface before it hardens. Work in small sections at a time. Try to lay as flat a surface as possible,

Above: *Mosaic-patterned stepping stones add splashes of colour through a lawn of aromatic chamomile and thyme. The herbs' scent will be released with each step.*

Right: *Terracotta-tiled steps edged with contrasting blue-grey lead to an hexagonal dais decorated with an intricate pebble mosaic.*

otherwise the floor will be uncomfortable to walk on. Pebbles and cobbles often have a distinct shape, being slightly flattened for example, and you can create interesting effects by laying adjacent sections of cobbles either flat or edge on. Contain concrete and pebble floors and pathways with tanalized gravel boards held in place with stout wooden pegs, or use a line of bricks, pavers or setts, or strips of marble if they are available, to create a firm boundary. You could use these same materials to create patterns, such as a brick diamond-shaped grid infilled with stones.

Laying Paving

A wide range of paving is suitable for the floor of your Mediterranean-inspired patio, from natural stone to smooth or riven concrete pavers. Look for lighter colours of sandstone, including types with pink and yellow shading, honey-coloured limestone or subtly shaded equivalents in reconstituted paving. A rectilinear paving design, using four or five different shapes and sizes, will suit larger, more formal patio settings. Include a proportion of much larger stone pieces to avoid the design becoming too 'busy', and consider working bricks or cobble panels into the design to soften the appearance.

In more rustic surroundings, small areas of paving could be laid using large, randomly shaped and somewhat rugged looking stone pieces set together 'crazy paving' style, perhaps leaving planting holes for aromatic herbs, such as thyme, oregano and Corsican mint. When trodden on, these creeping plants release a scent characteristic of the Mediterranean countryside. Avoid plain, dark coloured slate and other types of sombre grey stone, especially in shady areas, and instead look for pieces marbled with red and orange veins to add warmth.

Above: *Bold agave and rounded pebbles contrast with simple paving slabs.*

Choosing Tiles

Glazed ceramic or plain terracotta tiles have long been used to create floors in courtyards and gardens across the Mediterranean region. In cooler, wetter climates, take care to select tiles that are frostproof and that provide a reasonable grip in damp weather – a perfectly smooth surface can be lethally slippery when wet or frosty. Unless very well compacted, ground can shift fractionally, so ensure that tiles are thick enough to withstand the stress of being walked on when the foundation is slightly uneven. A smooth, even concrete slab makes an ideal base.

Ceramic tiles have an advantage over other paving types in being easier to sweep and wash over when dirty. This makes them ideal for walkways and outdoor cooking and dining areas. You can often match the tiling of a kitchen or conservatory with that of the patio to create a visual link.

Ceramic tiles also come in a wide range of colours. Browns and terracotta shades suit the Mediterranean style perfectly. Use other colours, such as ultramarine blue or lemon yellow sparingly and for dramatic effect. Nowadays,

Above: *Sliced roofing tiles and stone chips create intricate patterns.*

manufacturers tend to make mostly plain frostproof tiles and it is harder to track down patterns. You might, for example, wish to use a traditional Moorish design to create a border around a square of plain tiles for a Spanish-style patio. Complete Moroccan/Moorish tile panels are available from Internet stores, but if you visit reclamation yards you can often pick up Victorian tiles with suitable designs. In small, square or rectangular patios, or as a central focus for a larger site, combine tiles of different colours, shapes and sizes to create a Persian carpet effect, but ensure that the bulk of the 'carpet' is the same plain colour, perhaps rotated and laid on the diagonal for extra interest.

Mosaic Effects

As a focal point for your Mediterranean patio you might consider a Greco-Roman style mosaic using traditional tesserae – small squares of stone or ceramic tile. Complicated designs are a job for a mosaic artist, but simple designs combining tiles and

Left: *Areas surfaced solely with gravel can seem rather plain. To add texture and pattern, consider working in a design of quarry tiles or small square pavers, in warm shades of terracotta.*

Above: *Mini brick setts add extra texture to this curved edging.*

pebbles, for example, can be easy and effective. An example of this might be creating a replacement centre to a pre-cut paving stone circle. Some manufacturers provide such panels ready-made, featuring birds, animals and insects, or sun or star motifs.

Mediterranean patios are sometimes laid using a plain paving material incorporating a repeating pattern of mosaic-like elements, such as a flower or star motif. These elements may combine differently coloured pieces of precision-cut stone, terracotta or ceramic tile or polished marble.

TILE SHARDS FOR MOSAIC

• *Use coloured, patterned pieces to create decorative borders, panels or wandering lines within tiles or paving.*
• *Fix tile shards to a smooth concrete base using exterior-quality waterproof tile adhesive and grout.*
• *Extend the flowing patterns of tile shards in floors up on to walls and on the sides of raised beds.*
• *Create mosaic designs, such as simple flowers and stylized birds, with coloured glazed shards combined with pebbles or shells.*
• *Use broken floor tiles to surface paths between raised vegetable beds, creating a free-draining surface.*

MAKING A PEBBLE FLOOR MOSAIC

A small number of mosaic panels, perhaps laid to replace plain pavers, will produce a wonderfully textured and eye-catching surface, helping to emphasize the Mediterranean style. Using pebbles in a mosaic feature, instead of tesserae or tile shards, makes the process much easier. A panel like this can be completed in under an hour. Try out the design on an identically sized area first, so that you know how many of each type and size of pebble you need.

1 Lift a paving slab to accommodate your mosaic, or leave a gap when laying paving. Over a solid base of compacted hardcore add a layer of builders' sand. Tamp down with a block of wood and check that the surface is level.

2 Add a ready-made bag of dry mortar mix. Wear gloves to protect your hands from the lime and work from a kneeling pad for comfort. Check that the finished level once the pebbles are in place will be flush with the rest of the paving.

3 Find the centre of the panel by marking the intersection of two diagonal lines. Now start placing your pebbles in position, starting with the blue metallic marble, then add white, black and grey rings of pebbles.

4 Continue to build the design in rings, setting the smaller pebbles on edge to create an interesting texture. Use a piece of sawn timber and a rubber mallet to check that the surface of the pebbles is at the same level as the surrounding paving.

5 Select larger corner and edge pebbles in browns and paler greys and arrange to bridge the gap between the main circular block and the surrounding paving. These will be the guidelines for filling in the rest of the design.

6 Fill the remaining spaces with more pebbles, choosing appropriate sizes to fit the gaps. Keep the design as tightly packed as possible. You may need to replace pebbles with ones that are a better fit as you near completion.

7 Check levels again with the piece of timber and mallet. Work in more dry mortar mix using a nylon hand brush to tamp the material down in between the pebbles. This mix will set solidly, forming a durable and weather-resistant surface.

8 Fill a hand sprayer with water and use it to moisten the dry mortar mix and to reveal the protruding pebbles. Clean off excess mortar with the spray and a damp cloth, but don't disturb the pebbles and scrape away too much of the mortar.

9 The moistened mortar mix will eventually set. Cover it with plastic sheeting if rain threatens or if the weather is hot and dry. Because the pebbles are laid flush with the paving, you can walk over them with ease.

WALLS FOR MEDITERRANEAN SPACES

Introducing a Mediterranean design style may not be compatible with the surrounding architecture. If your patio is enclosed by something other than plain, rendered walls, you can achieve the right style of backdrop by employing different camouflage techniques and decorative treatments.

Above: *This grey stone wall is enlivened by the blue door and pots with pelargoniums.*

Paint Effects

Thick, textured masonry paint camouflages uneven walls that may be made up of combinations of brickwork, building blocks or patches of rendering. This can be spray-painted for speed, using a proprietary spray kit for masonry paint, or painted with a roller. If the patio is surrounded by high walls, you only need to paint to just above the ground floor windows and doors. This helps to define the outdoor space.

Though houses in hot, sunny regions frequently use white, in cool, wet climates this quickly discolours and looks too cold and stark under grey skies. Consider white with a touch of pink, green, pearl grey or sky blue, or choose authentic colours, such as terracotta or an evocative Moorish blue. Adjacent walls could be painted in

different hues and you could confine a more strident shade to just one wall, almost like a huge outdoor canvas.

Above: *Dusty terracotta wall tints, looking like aged plaster, provide a mellow and relaxing backdrop to this Mediterranean-style courtyard.*

Rendered Walls

For a backdrop, hide brickwork or breeze (cinder) blocks using a coat of cement render. Block walls can be given character by incorporating scattered pieces of rough stonework, a carved neo-classical corbel or a terracotta wall mask, or by creating niches and alcoves for candles and oil lamps. Work the rendering so the features blend in.

Left: *For a more rustic, weathered look, consider using wood stains rather than paints for woodwork.*

Right: *Use colour to emphasize contrast between inner and outer walls.*

CREATING A DUSTY TERRACOTTA WALL

On a plain rendered wall you can mimic the appearance of weathered plaster and create a more aged and established-looking backdrop for your patio or courtyard. This effect combines well with more rustic paving treatments, plain terracotta pots and elegant wirework furniture. While the example here shows soft brown and orange shades, you can also try blending blues and greens with touches of copper and bronze for a verdigris effect. Alternatively, roughly apply a deep blue or maroon red over a paler base coat.

1 Ensure that the rendered wall is sound. Remove any flaking paint and clean off cobwebs and grime. If necessary, seal the surface with a solution of PVA glue and allow it to dry before applying a white base coat. Paint over with a light terracotta-coloured emulsion.

2 Mix some darker coloured terracotta into the paint already in the tray, such as artist's acrylic or paint from a paint tester pot. Dab it on lightly with a piece of natural sponge to give a mottled effect.

3 Work the darker colour or colours over a larger area of the wall, softening and spreading the emulsion in a circular motion using a wallpaper pasting brush, a decorating brush, or a sponge as shown here.

4 Apply white emulsion or artist's acrylic randomly using a small paintbrush. Roll the brush in contact with the wall, drag it downwards or just touch the wall with the tip of the bristles.

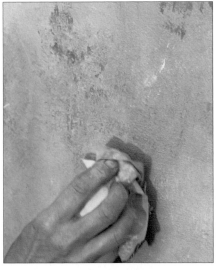

5 Continue to soften the darker and lighter shades using a rag or cloth to dab off excess or to add in colour. The white paint mimics salts that work their way to the surface. Once dry, weatherproof the wall using an exterior matt varnish. The different tones create texture, making the surface appear uneven and aged.

6 This backdrop is perfect for the mellow mood of a Mediterranean courtyard and makes a more suitable surface for displaying rustic ornaments, such as this ironwork candle lantern or a filigree Moorish screen.

Treillage for Flower-filled Walls

This style of decorative trelliswork, already mentioned in the Traditional Lines chapter (see page 16), can also be a feature in Mediterranean patios. The look is achieved using treillage panels carrying many small wall pots overflowing with flowers and foliage. Treillage panels can also break up the overly dominant impact of red- or buff-coloured brick walls and offer a stylish and relatively inexpensive makeover. Choose square or more ornate diamond trellis patterns, either with plain or curved tops to suit the mood. Fixing fence posts in between each panel creates the illusion that the trellis is freestanding and sets up a visual rhythm.

Screw the trellis to a framework of horizontal battens (leave a gap behind the panels, allowing room for climbers and wall shrubs). Consider painting the trellis a pale or vibrant colour to contrast with the brickwork and to bring the focus forward and away from the wall. You can strengthen the effect further by painting the wall behind using a light-reflecting shade of masonry paint.

Above: *Once a wall fountain, this window-shaped niche, bordered with decorative tiles and overflowing with pink pot geraniums, creates a strong focal point.*

Above: *This blue diamond trellis provides a framework for numerous wall pots.*

Above: *Paint walls to complement the colour of climbers such as this bougainvillea.*

Above: *Grow heat-loving alpines and drought-tolerant succulents in dry stone walls.*

Right: *Choose geraniums and other drought-tolerant patio plants with brightly coloured blooms for wall-planting schemes.*

Living Camouflage

Fixed wooden trellis panels or a framework of horizontal and vertical galvanized wire stretched between vine eyes for support, allow you to camouflage walls with foliage and flower. Lush, fast-growing climbers for a sunny patio include passion flower (*Passiflora caerulea*), flame-coloured Chilean glory vine (*Eccremocarpus scaber*) or the white or purple-flowered potato vines (*Solanum*). The evergreen *Clematis armandii*, with almond-scented, late-spring blooms and glossy leaves, looks suitably exotic, and jasmine and honeysuckle conjure images of sultry nights. Honeysuckle thrives in shade and works well with the self-clinging climbing hydrangea (*Hydrangea anomala* subsp. *petiolaris*) and cream variegated Algerian ivy (*Hedera canariensis* 'Gloire de Marengo').

Wall shrubs also contribute to the courtyard scene, especially when clipped to shape and tied in to stop them encroaching. The evergreen, honey-scented *Viburnum tinus* 'Eve

Above: *Reed or bamboo panels create a backdrop for a productive area.*

Price' flowers all winter and into spring. Clip as a half cone. For variegated leaves and a neat, rounded habit grow *Pittosporum tenuifolium* 'Abbotsbury Gold' or 'Silver Princess' and, tolerant of cooler conditions, *Rhamnus alaternus* 'Argenteovariegata'.

Creating Boundaries

The cost of a new brick or stone boundary wall might be prohibitive, but you can make relatively inexpensive walls from concrete building, or breeze (cinder) blocks. To integrate them, render the surface and paint it. Consider adding an appropriate coping stone or tile. Use a pitched topping of reclaimed terracotta pantiles, or a flat slate or reproduction terracotta-effect paving slab. If possible, work in architectural details such as buttressing and narrow window slots for interest.

Standard wooden fencing, especially when it is a mix of different styles, needs camouflaging in a Mediterranean patio with a uniform material, such as bamboo or reed fencing. This is available in rolls ready to attach to the fencing support behind using a heavy-duty staple gun. To create divisions within the patio – for an intimate dining area, for example – use the same materials ready-made into panels or trellis. Lightweight screens should only need an 8cm (3in) post. Fix the post into a metal socket for ease of replacement or when dealing with a concrete floor. Alternatively, consider using troughs with trellis attached to the back so that you can combine plants and introduce vibrant colour and fragrance. You can move these screen troughs around with ease if you attach castors to the bases.

PLANTS AND CONTAINERS FOR MEDITERRANEAN SPACES

Without doubt, the two most important elements in creating a Mediterranean patio are the plants and the pots you put them in. Terracotta is a signature material of the region, and plant species linked with an almost frost-free climate, such as grapevine, citrus, palms and succulents, define the look.

Above: *This large Cretan jar makes a dramatic focal point.*

Mediterranean-style Pots

Terracotta in all its forms is ideal for the Mediterranean-style courtyard. Look for containers marked with a frost-proof guarantee, rather than those described as 'frost resistant'. Good-quality pots are made from different kinds of clay and are fired at a higher temperature. Avoid pots with any obvious cracks or flaking. Gently knock the container with your knuckles and listen for a bell-like ringing tone. If you hear a dull thud, there may be a hairline crack. To conserve moisture loss, for plants other than those requiring sharp drainage, such as succulents, line terracotta pots with thin plastic, keeping the drainage hole uncovered. Matching pot feet raise the container, creating a more elegant appearance and improving drainage.

Above: *Recycled containers can be used for planters, as this hand-painted cistern shows, filled with zonal pelargoniums, pinks and trailing nepeta.*

Above: *An amphora in a metal stand becomes a planter for a pink begonia.*

You may need to protect ornately decorated terracotta and pots that are not guaranteed as frostproof through winter; wrap them in situ with plastic bubble wrap, greenhouse insulation fleece or with hessian stuffed with straw. Otherwise, move the pots to a frost-free position.

Simple, traditionally shaped pots can be combined with ease and will fit in with most schemes. The pale, dusty white patina of some is particularly suggestive of hot, dry gardens, but the shape and surface design make some pots more suited to Mediterranean settings. Ribbed olive jars (*pithoi*) taper to a narrow opening and are often impractical for planting – although their large size works well to 'anchor' a collection of

smaller pots or you can also convert one into a water feature. Amphorae have rounded bases and handles and are usually displayed in a metal stand, although you can lay them on the ground and plant them with succulents seeming to pour out of their mouth. Both of these pot types work well in Greco-Roman, Moorish or Greek island-style settings. For a garden with influences from the Italian Renaissance or the Riviera, add a few more ornately decorated pots and planters, urns and vases. While in more rustic gardens, a

Above: *Plain terracotta pots and planters house a large cineraria (Senecio cineraria) in a signature pot and zonal pelargoniums.*

Succulents and Cacti

While you may garden in cool temperate or maritime climes with plentiful rainfall, incorporating some drought-adapted plants will help to create the illusion of dry heat in your patio. Plants that can stay out all year include house leeks, or *Sempervivum*, and the similar looking *Jovibarba*. Both are called hen and chicks because of their creeping colonies, the parent plant being surrounded by the smaller offsets. Grow them in shallow pots filled with sharply draining compost (soil mix) or work them into paving and wall cracks and crevices.

Most creeping alpine sedum or stonecrop species and cultivars are also hardy and evergreen if they are given good drainage. Plants such as the dusty blue-white *Sedum* 'Cape Blanco' and the deep purple-red

Above: Sempervivum *(house leeks) make a fine collection for a ceramic trough.*

Sedum spurium 'Red Carpet' add to the colour palette. If you are looking to enhance your green credentials, any of these types of plant can also be used to create living roof coverings for sheds and other garden buildings.

jumbled collection of cheaper containers, such as old olive oil cans, is often seen clustered together and painted in the same sky blue or peppermint as the doors and shutters.

PLANTING AN AGAVE

Succulents, such as this sculptural *Agave americana*, make wonderful pot specimens, but they need a special planting method to keep them healthy. Good drainage is critical. Plants can remain in their pots for several years as they don't mind being pot bound, but during the summer months they will benefit from regular watering and feeding.

In winter, drastically reduce watering and move the plant under cover, standing in a bright, frost-free place such as an unheated conservatory. Or if that's not possible, move to the shelter of overhanging evergreens or to the base of a sunny wall, where plants will be protected from frost and kept relatively dry.

1 The terracotta jar has a Spanish or Moorish feel but its narrow neck means that it will have to be broken when the agave needs to be extracted for repotting. Place a crock or a stone over the drainage hole to prevent the compost (soil mix) from blocking it.

2 Mix ordinary soil-based potting compost with a quantity of horticultural grit to ensure good drainage. Overly wet soil can cause the roots to rot and sharp drainage helps plants survive when winter temperatures fall.

3 Add some of the mixture to the pot and try the plant for size. The soil surface should sit a little below the pot rim to allow for watering. Work in more potting mix to fill gaps around the root-ball (roots). Firm the compost lightly. Water well. Stand the pot on 'feet' to ensure free drainage.

Other Succulent Options

A surprisingly diverse range of succulents survives year round within the sheltered environs of a townhouse or sunny walled patio, especially if pots are kept virtually dry through winter. Try the beautifully sculpted rosettes of *Echeveria* and *Hawarthia* as well as gasterias, crassulas and Aloe species and cultivars. The latter often have vibrant orange or salmon-pink flower spires.

Architectural succulents that make eye-catching pot specimens, but which will almost certainly need overwintering in a conservatory, are the century plant *Agave americana* (see potting sequence on page 43) and the almost black-leaved *Aeonium* 'Zwartkop'. Also consider the prickly pear cactus *Opuntia*, with its flattened, oval-shaped segments.

Floral Sights and Scents

The wild Mediterranean landscape gives off a pungent cocktail of aromatic oils and you can pick out the different scents from pine trees as well as carpeting herbs and shrubs, such as artemisia, thyme, oregano,

Above: *Herbs and sun-loving aromatic plants, such as lavender and Moroccan mint, add a touch of the wild Mediterranean.*

sage, rosemary, lavender, Cistus (rock rose) and *Phlomis fruticosa* (Jerusalem sage). Use variegated and coloured-leaf herbs as a foil for flowering plants wherever possible and be sure to site lavender, rosemary and the tender wall shrub lemon verbena (*Aloysia triphylla*) close to doorways and sitting areas, where a cloud of fragrance will be released every time the foliage is brushed past. Similarly work in the fruity-scented chamomile, pungent thymes and Corsican mint into paving cracks.

As well as the evening-scented jasmine, honeysuckle and four o'clock plant, or marvel of Peru (*Mirabilis jalapa*), try using wisteria over archways and pergolas so that its fragrant blooms hang down just above head height. Climbing roses would also be in keeping.

A riot of colourful flowering plants grown in pots is typical of Mediterranean patios. Include classics such as pelargoniums and decorate patios with marguerite daisies, osteospermums, mop-head hydrangeas, lilies and flame-coloured gazania and arctotis. Australasian flowering shrubs are increasingly popular, ranging from *Callistemon* (bottle brush) to more unusual plants, such as *Metrosideros*

Above: *An impressive row of potted* Agave *tops this courtyard wall, adding a distinctly sub-tropical feel.*

and *Grevillea*. With a conservatory you can more easily overwinter tender and borderline hardy shrubs and tuberous rooted plants such as the velvet purple *Tibouchina semidecandra*, fragrant angel's trumpets *(Brugmansia)* and Indian shot *(Canna)*.

Above: *A large terracotta pot, lined with plastic, can house permanent plantings such as a vine or bay standard.*

TRAINING A GRAPEVINE

The vine shown growing in an Italianate terracotta pot on the opposite page (below right) has been trained in a version of the single-curtain system. Its support is the stout pier of the loggia and the horizontal branches run just under the roofline. When the vine fruits, bunches of grapes will hang down. Use a John Innes soil-based potting compost (soil mix) with added well-rotted manure as the plant will be in position for several years.

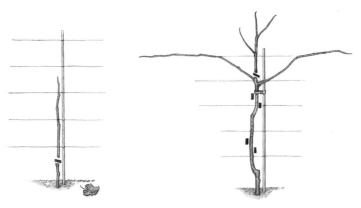 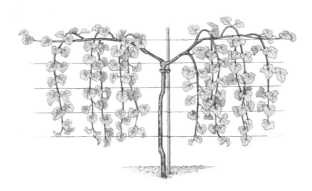

1 Start with a one-year-old vine planted in winter and cut through the leader about 15cm (6in) above the ground.
In summer, tie in the new leader as it develops. In the following winter, cut back the leader again, this time removing half of the previous year's growth. Tie in the leader as it develops and continue this process until you reach the desired height.

2 In the third year during mid-winter, remove all the laterals (side shoots) on the main stem except for the two positioned just below the wire support. Bend these out and tie them in to the horizontal wires. In the summer, side shoots on these two main laterals will develop and hang down, to form the characteristic hanging vine shape.

3 Allow the hanging shoots to develop every 30cm (12in). Pinch out the side shoots. Prune established plants in winter, cutting back all the hanging shoots to one or two upward-facing buds and allowing one shoot to develop on the previous year's spurs. Thin bunches of grapes for bigger fruits.

Sculptural Highlights

Palms, such as the hardy Chusan fan palm, *Trachycarpus fortunei*, and borderline hardy Mediterranean fan palm, *Chamaerops humilis*, add real drama with their large, exotic-looking leaves. Tree ferns produce a similar look in shady corners, especially when the 'trunk' is well developed.

For a leafy fountain effect, grow the cabbage palm *(Cordyline australis)*. The plain-leaved version is remarkably hardy given good winter drainage and eventually forms a small tree. This familiar patio pot plant comes in purple shaded or variegated leaf forms, which can survive year to year given virtually frost-free conditions. A tougher choice for more exposed gardens is the New Zealand flax *(Phormium tenax)*. This produces bold tufts of strap-shaped leaves and is not fussy about soil. There are scores of

Above: *Spiky* Cordyline australis *adds bold vertical accents to this 'hot' border.*

Above: *For living sculpture try the impressive flower spike of* Yucca gloriosa.

purple, yellow, copper pink and variegated forms, but these are not as tough as the species – although they do make spectacular potted specimens. The spear-shaped leaves

of yuccas also catch the eye, especially bold-yellow variegated forms, such as *Yucca gloriosa* 'Variegata' and *Y. filamentosa* 'Bright Edge'.

STRUCTURES AND FURNITURE FOR MEDITERRANEAN SPACES

The relaxed Mediterranean lifestyle revolves around sitting, eating and cooking alfresco, and structures such as pergolas and loggias are essential additions. Most patios are simply furnished. Add plain wooden seats and create a focus with a mosaic- or marble-topped table to help set the mood.

Above: *Create a casual style with mismatched furniture and fabrics.*

Left: *The eye-catching blue and terracotta walls of this pergola-shaded seating area, coupled with architectural plantings, creates a wonderful Mediterrancean ambience.*

Above: *This pergola, entwined with a well-established wisteria, provides welcome shade on a sunny Mediterranean terrace.*

Shade from the Sun

While not exclusive to the Mediterranean garden, pergolas fit beautifully with the style and give welcome shade in a sunny patio in which to sit and relax. Freestanding or attached to a wall, a timber pergola could be covered with inexpensive reed matting during the summer to give instant dappled shade. Remove it towards the end of the year to allow more light in, vital in cooler, cloudier regions. For the same reason, it is advisable to plant with deciduous climbers, such as grapevines, rambler roses, wisteria, potato vine and jasmine.

You can buy straightforward kits from garden centres and home-improvement stores but consider using reclaimed wood for rustic appeal. On existing concrete floors fix pergola posts by bolting on metal sockets (see method page 135). Avoid ornate trellis additions and make sure there is sufficient head height once climbers have grown, otherwise pergolas can feel claustrophobic. Starting with a 2.5m (8ft) clearance usually gives enough room for the foliage. Heavy uprights, including those made from natural stone or rendered blocks, and weighty cross beams give a feeling of robustness to the structure.

The Italian loggia – an open-fronted roofed area built against a wall – provides an all-weather spot from which to enjoy the garden. Covering the slanting roof with weathered terracotta pantiles and using uprights made from reclaimed oak or hardwood beams creates the illusion of age. Consider painting the interior wall white or a pale pastel shade to reflect the light and lay decorative tiles or perhaps cobbles on the floor.

Some courtyards are large enough to accommodate a small timber summerhouse, especially one designed for a corner position. Again, replacing a plain roofing felt covering with terracotta tiles helps the building look more authentic. Select a timber stain or exterior quality paint to evoke a Mediterranean mood, such as

Right: *An angled framework of overhead timbers and wire supports a grapevine that offers dappled shade in summer when* Trachelospermum *scents the air.*

cornflower blue, a good background shade for terracotta. Buildings such as this could house and camouflage a spa pool, where the more usual Nordic design log cabin would feel out of place.

An off-the-peg wooden shed might not look ideal in your Mediterranean patio, but storage space in small gardens is often a problem. You could build a concrete-block lean-to with rendered walls, a reclaimed wooden door and a roof planted with succulents. Also build storage compartments into low, rendered walls, using hinged wooden seats for access.

Outdoor Dining

In Mediterranean gardens it is quite common to find a simple charcoal barbecue grate built against a wall, with an adjacent log store, and you could also fit a traditional whitewashed log-fired oven with chimney if space allows. A built-in wall cupboard might house

crockery and glasses, herbs and seasonings, and the low walls of raised beds could be converted to make a casual seating area.

A large, tiled dining table, made from substantial reclaimed timbers or a block of stone, could be left outside all year round. Selected with care, such a table could act as a sculptural focal point. In summer, surround the table with a mismatched collection of kitchen chairs, some with woven wicker seats, to help create the more informal look of a Greek taverna.

Left: *A simple serving and dining area close to the back door encourages alfresco cooking and eating.*

Where space is limited, choose a small, square or circular café-style table with foldaway chairs. Metal-framed tables with mosaic tops are perfect for an Italian- or Moorish-style. You can also find marble-topped tables with heavy cast-iron bases.

Wirework tables and chairs add a touch of elegance and give character to a period-style courtyard, one that perhaps harks back to Edwardian times. Weathered Lloyd Loom armchairs also work well surrounded by lush, potted foliage and flowers. Ornate, black, wrought ironwork is reminiscent of Venetian houses and dining suites with glass-topped tables are perfect for more sophisticated Mediterranean settings. Avoid standing ironwork on paving or you risk rust stains appearing.

Wood is warm to the touch, unlike metal, and whether you are perched on a Moroccan-carved stool sipping mint tea or stretched out on a vintage-style steamer chair you can appreciate its natural beauty. Wooden furniture varies in style from a rough-hewn bench made from driftwood to a classic hardwood table and chairs set, complete with colonial-style canvas sunshade. Tropical or temperate hardwood,

sourced from sustainable plantations, is very durable, but for a greener alternative look locally for furniture made from reclaimed materials. In Mediterranean regions you will often see household furniture, such as a farmhouse-style kitchen table, used outdoors and it is possible to find furniture like this second-hand.

Wicker or cane pieces are not weatherproof, but could be used in a summerhouse or loggia. If you like

Above: *The combination of mosaic tiling on the table surface and scrolled wrought iron work adds a flavour of Italy to this courtyard dining space.*

the informal look of wicker, painted or natural, consider wicker substitutes made from UV-stabilized acrylic. Cheaper designs are coated with colour and can start to show wear: more expensive models are coloured throughout.

Above: *This simple mosaic tabletop features a blue themed geometric design.*

Above: *A serene space, covered in dappled shade from the vine-covered pergola, has been created with a stone table and bench suite and a decorative tiled floor.*

HOW TO MAKE A MOSAIC TABLE-TOP

The combination of Mediterranean colours and the simple design of this mosaic table creates a striking piece of furniture. Made from 13mm- (½in-) thick marine or exterior-grade plywood, the table can be used outdoors in good weather, but you will need to bring it inside during sustained rainy periods and for the winter. As an alternative to this simple floral design you could create more abstract patterns without using a template. For example, you could sketch a series of waves going across a square or oblong table-top or simply build up a series of concentric rings, varying in width, using the different shades for contrast.

1 Mark out the table circumference using a piece of string tied to a drawing pin at the centre of the plywood and a pencil at the other. Cut out with a jigsaw. Trace your chosen design on to tracing paper, going over the lines thickly with a soft pencil.

2 Turn the tracing paper on top of the plywood so that the pencil lines are facing down. Line up the template with the centre and rub over the lines with a pencil to transfer the pattern. Seal the board, including the rim, with diluted PVA glue.

3 Using tile nippers, and wearing goggles, cut the glass mosaic tiles into halves and thirds so that you have a variety of different widths. Make a small pile of each of the colours. Save some whole tiles to nibble into different sizes and shapes later.

4 Mix up waterproof tile adhesive and, using a flexible knife, spread it over one area of the design at a time, approximately 3mm (⅛in) thick. Select shards in four colours, pressing them into the adhesive. Leave a small gap between pieces.

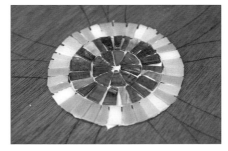

5 Prepare the next area for tiling, wiping off any adhesive spillages immediately. Fill in the area inside the ring with two colours of the mosaic pieces. In order to achieve a neat finish in the design, nibble the tiles into wedge shapes.

6 Following the same technique, begin to fill out the rounded petals. Outline the petals first with a rim of tile shards and then begin infilling. For this element of the design use the paler tiles. Nibble shards to fit the gaps neatly.

7 Begin filling in the pointed petals with darker contrasting tile shards. Fill the gaps in between the petals and table edge as well as the rim with the palest shades and leave it to dry for a day.

8 Wearing rubber gloves, mix up the grout in a bucket. Work the grout into all the gaps between the mosaic pieces using a tiler's spreader. Wipe over the table top and rim with a damp sponge to remove excess grout. Finally, polish with a soft, dry cloth.

9 When dry, turn the table-top over and spread the base with PVA glue. Allow it to dry. Mix up tile adhesive and spread it over the base evenly to seal it. Once dry, attach the table top to a metal table base frame using screws.

ORNAMENT AND WATER FEATURES FOR MEDITERRANEAN SPACES

In Mediterranean gardens, decoration and ornament are often provided by structural elements – mosaic floors, ironwork grilles and painted shutters, as well as smaller household pieces. Pots and planters, furniture or light fittings also play a decorative role and rills, raised pools and fountains create eye-catching flourishes.

Above: *A simple water carrier provides a pleasing poolside focus.*

Moorish Influence

There are numerous elements with subtle or overt references to the Moorish style: rendered walls painted to create a worn terracotta feel; a distinctive arched doorway or wall aperture; a carved wooden screen; or an ornate tile panel. Water features might include a formal rill, a carved marble or resin reproduction fountain or a mosaic pool. The latter can be decorated simply using mosaic sheets applied to a concrete base with waterproof tiling grout (waterproof as well as frost resistant). The individual square tiles, or tesserae, are held together by a mesh. You just need to work the grout into the gaps with a grouting tool and wipe the excess off.

Additional touches come in the choice of furniture, planters, fabrics and lighting. Consider a Moroccan hexagonal table made from intricately carved wood with matching stools; a large engraved brass water carrier or wall mounted tray; Moroccan metal lanterns and richly coloured cushions and throws.

Typical Decorative Features

Mediterranean gardens are full of pots and planters, and these provide numerous opportunities for decoration. Used sparingly, large pithoi and amphora, terracotta vases and jars act as simple focal points. Even broken pots look the part when their remains are colonized with encrusting succulents.

As well as painting walls to create a distressed look, you could stencil a design with an oiled manilla stencil design and acrylic paint. Rub over parts of the painted areas with sandpaper to give a weathered effect.

You can also hang wall plaques to enhance your chosen style, including terracotta or metalwork sun emblems, which work well in simple and more rustic-looking whitewashed patios. Wrought-iron grilles aged by rusting can be purchased from garden centres. Set these in small window apertures knocked through the boundary walls or set them above a garden gate. Alternatively, fix a grille to a wall using a mirror behind to create the illusion of light streaming through. Finish by planting a colourful window box or wall planter beneath.

Neo-classical wall masks and terracotta friezes would suit an Italian-style courtyard and you could also set a small statue, bust or oil lamp in a wall niche or on a carved stone corbel cemented on to the wall.

Above: *A wall niche raises the profile of smaller decorative objects.*

Above: *Look out for salvaged ironwork pieces that can be integrated.*

Above: *Quirky mosaic wall art feels perfectly at home in a relaxed patio.*

Above: *A small fountain is made more prominent by the mosaic floor treatment.*

Left: *The brick arch, trained with climbers, and plain rendered wall help to frame this water sculpture.*

reservoir below rather than into a pool. If you have the room and want to fill the space with the sight and sound of water, build a long, narrow pool fitted with arcing water jets, reminiscent of the Alhambra in Spain. Be aware, however, that the sound of running water can become intrusive and it may not be as relaxing as you first imagine!

Above: *A Moorish tiled pool with palms and a trickling fountain cools the air.*

Water Features

There's often very little floor room in a patio and so a wall-mounted water feature, such as self-contained terracotta wall fountain or a wall spout emptying into a rectangular or semi-circular wall pool, is ideal. Designs can be adapted depending on the style you want to achieve. In a Moorish setting, consider tiling the pool and surround in a deep blue; for a Greek-island feel, render the raised pool and walls and create a seat using terracotta paving tiles.

A fountain at the centre of a tiny shaded patio brings light and movement. Keep the design simple and where space is limited have the water tumbling down into a hidden

WATER GARDEN TIPS

• *Camouflage electrical wiring and water pipes to wall fountains and self-contained features using loose cobbles, plants and climbers.*
• *Adjust the water outlet of pumps to create a gentle trickling sound, or use stones to disperse the water stream before it hits the reservoir.*
• *Use as large a hidden reservoir as possible with a plastic sheet surround to minimize water loss.*

Safety note: *Take precautions to prevent children having access to ponds or other water features.*

BUILDING A RILL

In a Mediterranean-style patio, especially if it has a Spanish or Moorish feel, a shallow canal or rill may be used to emphasize a formal layout or to create a strong central axis. The long, narrow water surface can look like a thread of mercury, reflecting the sky, especially in a shaded patio, and makes the most of the available natural light. The source of a rill can become an important decorative addition and in the illustration below, a terracotta pot surrounded by plants is an easily copied example.

1 Construct a reservoir that is large enough to contain all the shallow water in the rill at the point where the rill discharges the water. Place a submersible pump in the water-filled reservoir and position a paving stone over the top to keep out light and debris.

2 Construct a shallow watertight trench using a flexible liner and concrete shuttering along the proposed route of the rill.

3 Bury a corrugated, flexible delivery pipe at a shallow depth alongside the concrete rill to deliver the water to the source point, in this case a terracotta pot. The flexible pipe (available in different diameters from water garden specialists) fits on to the submersible pump outlet and the other end pushes in through the drainage hole of the pot. It doesn't need to be a perfect fit as the water pools into the base of the urn below the hole. It is especially important, if the end of the rill is not next to a wall, to camouflage the inlet point using lush plantings or a collection of planted pots.

4 When the pump is working, the water bubbles up inside the pot and overflows into the rill, trickling back to the reservoir. Levels will need topping up from time to time as the water evaporates.

Top right: *This view shows how water is automatically recycled from the reservoir housing the pump, through the urn and out into the channel.*

Above right: *A rill requires firm foundations to prevent slumping or cracking due to poorly consolidated ground.*

Right: *Simple stepping-stone 'bridges' allow easy access across the rill, from one part of the garden to another.*

MEDITERRANEAN RILL SIDE VIEW

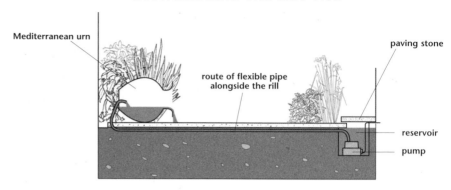

MEDITERRANEAN RILL CROSS-SECTION

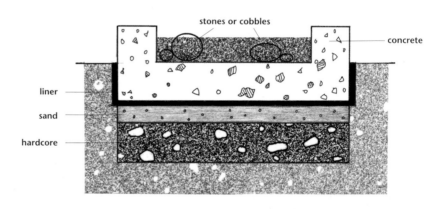

CREATING AN OVERFLOWING URN

Self-contained water features, such as this bubbling urn, are ideal for small gardens where there is insufficient space for a pool. They are child-friendly and because the pump is low voltage, running off a transformer, they are safe to install. A project such as this could be completed in just a few hours.

1 Select a suitably styled terracotta pot that fits in with your patio. Apply several coats of diluted PVA sealant inside and out. This will frost-proof the urn and also allow the water to flow over the sides more evenly.

2 The urn has been sited in a raised bed. Raising a feature above ground level makes it more prominent. If the patio has a concrete base, you may have to build up around the feature rather than digging down. Dig out most of the soil.

3 Remove sharp stones, line the hole with pond or carpet underlay and cover with an off-cut of butyl rubber pond liner. Fold a piece of underlay or liner to cushion the pile of bricks that will support the urn. Cement these together.

4 Ensure that the bricks are level using a small spirit level and cover the hole with galvanized mesh. Overlap the edges to provide maximum support. Using wire cutters, snip a hole in the mesh to accommodate the submersible pump.

5 Put the pump into the cistern, feeding the wire up through the mesh at the back of the bed. Plug the pump into a transformer situated in a waterproof housing or inside a building. Check all connections with a qualified electrician.

6 Drill a drainage hole in the urn to accommodate a 10mm (½in) water-tank coupler. Or, fix a rigid 10mm (½in) copper delivery tube in the urn, cutting it level with the rim of the pot. Seal the junction with the flexible pipe.

7 You can dismantle a water-tank coupler without breaking the watertight seal. Place the urn on the brick plinth, feeding the flexible tube through the slot in the top and down through the gaps to hold it in place. Connect it to the pump outlet.

8 Fill the reservoir and use the pump outlet adjuster to moderate the flow through the copper pipe. Turn down the jet so that it bubbles slightly above the water's surface. Cover the mesh with landscape membrane to filter out debris. Camouflage with cobbles.

LIGHTING FOR MEDITERRANEAN SPACES

It can be a relaxing ritual in the sheltered confines of a patio to light all the tea lights and candles as day turns to night. The flickering light of candle lanterns and oil lamps creates the authentic ambience of a Mediterranean-style patio. For convenience and safety, think about suitable electric lights.

Above: *White fairy lights shine through a coloured glass fish.*

Left: *Verdigris-coloured coach lamps provide general lighting for the terrace while pendant uplighters illuminate the climbers.*

Lighting Ideas

Your choice of light depends on what you are trying to create: a shady oasis, like that found in the centre of a traditional Marrakech home; a simple Greek island-style courtyard or the sophisticated elegance of the terrace of an Italian villa.

To add a chic feel to a patio with plain rendered walls and simple floor tiles, try placing shallow, jewel-coloured glass tea-light holders in wall niches and on ledges or around the rim of a raised pool. Similar coloured-glass jar candle lanterns with simple wire handles allow you to hang lights from a pergola or tree branches. And for a starlit effect, weave tiny white fairy lights through climbers and wall shrubs covering the walls. Often the simplest ideas are the most contemporary in effect. Try chunky beeswax or church candles in unadorned terracotta pots. Hold them in place or at the right height with sand, fine gravel or coloured glass chippings and set among the plants or space them evenly along the base of a wall.

Intricately cut brass or silvery coloured metal lanterns are a signature of North Africa. When lit, they throw shadow patterns on to the walls, creating a magical ambience. If you are using traditional-style carved wooden or ironwork furniture, mosaic-topped tables and Moorish tiling details, these will be the perfect finishing touch. You can also buy ceramic lanterns with a similar cutwork design. Simple metallic brass and copper oil and gel lamps suit this style of patio, especially ones set in wrought-iron tripod stands or those designed to be hung from chains.

For a creative effect, backlight a decorative ironwork screen or illuminate a wooden treillage panel, hiding the lamp with a foreground of lush foliage plants. Architectural specimens, including palms, phormiums and tree ferns, will throw dramatic shadows on the walls when lit from below or from the side.

SAFETY NOTE

Don't leave naked flames unattended and ensure that lamps and lanterns are positioned safely. They can become hot and should be moved with care.

Above: *Coloured glass lanterns cast a gentle light and add to the Mediterranean theme.*

Wall Lights

The Venetians left an architectural legacy throughout the Mediterranean region, and elegant, black wrought-iron wall lamps with scrolling detail would suit a traditional Italian style courtyard adorned with terracotta pots, clipped bay topiary and potted olive trees. Most are designed for electric lighting, but some wall-mounted candle lanterns reminiscent of the period are also available. Rusting ironwork or weathered copper verdigris effects create an atmosphere of faded elegance and would work with more rustic features and older style properties. Going back to classical times, torch-style ironwork lamps add a touch of theatre, perfect for an outdoor dining room, and there are some surprisingly effective electric versions available. Ironwork candle sconces and candelabras are a luxurious indulgence and they can often be found in designs to match wall lights.

Highlighting Sculpture

Inconspicuous black or brushed-metal minispot uplighters are invaluable for throwing light on to sculptures, pots and water features and should be set into the ground or paving to make them even less

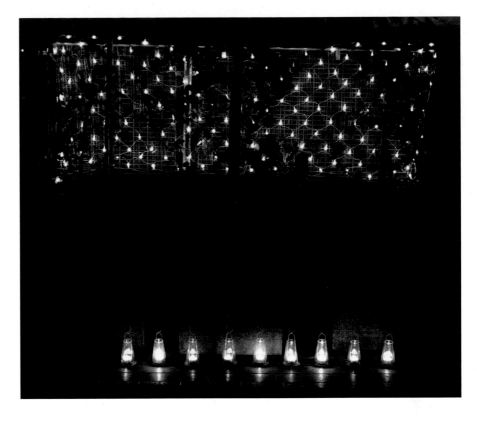

obtrusive. Used with restraint, they can subtly transform the look of the garden at night and make the most of design touches that might fade into the background during the day, especially in shady corners.

Uplighting from the side emphasizes the three-dimensional form of a sculpture to best effect. But a classical bust or wall mask might be more dramatic lit directly from below.

Above: *A net of low energy LEDs mimics light coming through a Moorish fretwork screen.*

Below left: *These curved ironwork lamps echo the Venetian style that is found throughout the Mediterranean.*

Below: *A traditional Moroccan lantern such as this adds the finishing touch to a Moorish courtyard.*

LIVING OUTDOORS

Tailoring an exterior space to work as a personal living space creates a halfway house between inside and outside. Treated in this way the patio garden is no longer a separate space, but more of an extension of the home, adjoining it and taking its theme and style from the furniture and decoration indoors. It is a place to relax and to entertain, and a green oasis for escape and refuge.

This room can be for pottering or playing, dining or debating. It can display a collection of artworks or be a habitat for wildlife. The theatrical potential of an outdoor room comes to the fore after sundown, when lighting can create an air of mystery and romance. How pleasant on a balmy evening to sit with friends around a candlelit supper table knowing that you can curl up later in a swing-seat under the stars, soothed by the sound of music or water in the background. Eating outside, surrounded by the calm and fragrance of foliage and flowers, is a marvellously simple way to enjoy your garden.

Left: *A bold timber pergola serves to create this intimate dining terrace, defining the space and providing a sense of enclosure without blocking the view to the garden beyond. Wooden furniture reinforces this strong but simple theme.*

FLOORING FOR OUTDOOR ROOMS

Galvanizing the overall 'look' of a space depends enormously on the flooring. This is the controlling factor in delineating space and also for creating colour, texture and mood. Although at first it may seem that the inside and outside are really separate spaces, in fact it is possible to make a truly fluid transition between the two.

Above: *A dramatic flooring feature made from curved sections of exotic hardwood.*

Choosing Materials

There are many materials suitable for exterior paving – wooden decking, natural stone, brick, fabricated slabs or gravel. Suitability for purpose should always be of paramount importance. Weight may be a consideration, especially with a roof terrace or balcony. Ease of access and portability are also important when building materials have to be taken through the house.

Wooden Floors

The first consideration when selecting flooring material is how to continue the textural theme of your interior. Wooden floors, currently a popular choice for interiors, can easily be made to float naturally through to the exterior, extending that warm ambience that works so well with a naturalistic planting scheme. The transition does require the use of an appropriate timber, one that will withstand the extremes of weather conditions, including rain, sun and frost.

Hardwoods are extremely durable and beautiful, requiring minimum maintenance. Tropical timbers, such as teak and iroko, are at the high end of quality and price, the former having a smooth, long-grained texture. In the case of all hardwoods check the supplies come from sustainable sources. Oak is an excellent choice, although it must be well seasoned to remove tannins that can stain surrounding materials. Hardwoods may be sealed with a varnish, giving them a deeper tone, or left to age to a sober, silvery grey.

Softwoods are well priced, but less durable. They must be pressure treated with a preservative, but even then have a tendency to distort and twist away from fixings.

There are economic, practical alternatives to hardwoods: Western red cedar and (to a lesser degree) Southern yellow pine have a natural durability, due to their rot-resisting resins, as well as an innate structural strength.

Timber becomes very slippery in regions of high rainfall so should be brushed and jet washed regularly to remove algae. Ribbed surface finishes are available to reduce the problem.

Wooden decking has increased in popularity, but it has too often been chosen as a cheap shortcut. This has been to the detriment of many spaces that would have been better served by traditional hard landscaping. Decking does fulfil certain requirements supremely well: it is useful when building raised areas to introduce changes of level and for transitions between different types of materials; and it makes an excellent pathway alongside water and through areas of natural planting.

Above: *A raised timber dining plinth gives focus and interest to a small terrace.*

Above: *A steep descent of steps with sawn timber is enclosed by retaining walls.*

Above: *Decking panels provide an easy way to cover up an unsightly solid floor.*

MAKING SIMPLE DECKING

You can find all the elements for creating a simple deck at larger DIY stores, including pre-cut, interlocking joists. Use pressure-treated timber supports and raise them off the ground to prevent rot. The simplest decks require minimal cutting. Consider the length of decking planks and avoid designs with multiple angles or curves.

1 Consolidate the area, and position concrete blocks or beams to support bearers. Set these on concrete foundations (on soft ground) ensuring they are level.

2 Treat cut ends with preservative. Use landscape membrane to prevent weeds as shown. Drill and screw the framework together at 40cm (16in) intervals.

3 Lay the decking boards across the joists. Secure with galvanized nails. Leave a gap of 6mm (1/4in) between boards for drainage and to allow wood to swell.

DECKING PATTERNS

Decking boards can be laid in a wide variety of patterns, (a) being the most simple. Prefabricated deck squares (b) are easy to lay (see also picture opposite). Designs on the diagonal are dynamic and include the chevron pattern (c) which is one of the more contemporary in effect, (d) a simpler version that can effectively 'point' like an arrow to a focal point, and (e), still stylish but within the capabilities of most enthusiastic amateurs. Design (f) is static and creates a calm atmosphere. If you want more texture, try the simple-to-lay interlocking design (g) or, for real flair, the diagonally cut version (h). Use recessed deck lights to emphasize deck patterns.

a

b

c

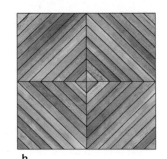

d

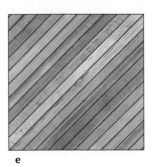

e

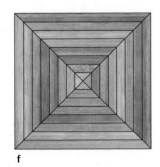

f

g

h

Left: *A soft and sinuous design is achieved with curvaceously cut, pale stone paving. Loops of darker stone provide relief detail.*

plain tiling can also be broken up using edging and details in a contrasting yet sympathetic material. Marble slips would be ideal for this as they are normally too fragile to be used outside as a walking surface. Tiles are available in a kaleidoscope of beautiful colours, making them ideal for intricate mosaic features. These make excellent focal points to enliven a neutral surface area or they can be used as border details to edge or highlight a path.

Natural stone is a popular choice for interior floor surfaces, especially in kitchens where its tactile qualities add to the creative environment. Pale limestone produces a restrained elegance, and this can be continued through to a terrace, reinforcing the cool and understated style. Slate, which, depending on its source, can be found in subtle, mossy tones and sober greys, provides a similarly restrained effect. Both have a contemporary, minimalist appearance when saw-cut and smoothly finished.

Linking Spaces

Kitchen and service areas are often the transition point to the garden and so provide a good place from which to develop your decorating scheme and extend into the outdoor room. For practical reasons, outdoor flooring materials may have to be adjusted, but the colour and texture can be carried through to make the passage appear seamless.

Tiling and Paving

A popular floor finish for kitchens, tiles are available in both ceramic and terracotta versions. However, it is essential that exterior flooring is weatherproof and, most importantly in the case of tiles, frost resistant. Natural terracotta works well indoors but tends to be porous and ceramic tiles are usually quite thin. High-fired exterior ceramic tiles can echo a Mediterranean or rustic look, and they have the advantage that out of doors they will not absorb water. Therefore, they will be less susceptible to damage caused by

freezing and subsequent thawing. Outdoor floor tiles must also be slip resistant, so always check this with the supplier before ordering.

Tiling over a large area can look hard and somewhat monotonous, so it is a good idea to create an interesting tile pattern. Areas of

Above: *A raised timber plinth creates a gentle transition from this garden bath house.*

Above: *Informal stone slabs surrounded by aromatic herbs makes an intriguing footway.*

Right: *Small-scale materials such as mosaic and brick help to achieve complicated designs like this curving, eastern style feature.*

Paving slabs manufactured from concrete are available in a wide variety of shapes, colours and textures, some echoing classical *trompe l'oeil* flooring designs. These can work well with traditional buildings and are considerably cheaper than natural materials.

Brick Floors

A popular construction material for centuries, brick is becoming more widely used as a facing material. With this style of building, brick pavers would make a sympathetic contribution to a flooring design. Pavers are versatile, and being small in size they can be laid in a variety of patterns (see also page 84). Brick can be used as an accent detail to add interest to a large expanse of stone paving and is invaluable in creating steps and low walls. Old, reclaimed wall bricks can have a warm texture, but they are completely unsuitable for use in paving. To avoid the risk of frost damage, it is important to use highly fired engineering bricks with low water porosity.

Above: *Old red bricks in a basketwork design lend a soft foundation to this terrace.*

Other Options

When a solid flooring material is out of the question, loose-laid gravel or stones may be the best option. The effect is informal and reminiscent of Mediterranean terraces, making an easy relationship with perennial planting and a cottage-style effect. Here it is entirely appropriate to use old bricks to create an edging detail for the planting beds.

Gravel is readily available, inexpensive and simple to lay. It can be found in various grades from tiny sharp fragments to large, smooth, rounded pebbles and cobbles that can be employed in beach-style features. Colours vary from white and grey to warm ochre and buff, enabling it to be used in a wide range of contexts.

To lay gravel, start with a simple foundation of compacted hardcore followed by a layer of medium-grade gravel mixed with a little dry cement. Water this in to achieve a weed-resistant barrier and then finish off with a thicker layer of finishing gravel. You can

CREATING A FOUNDATION

A secure foundation is required before laying any type of floor slab or tile. A level concrete base laid over a well-compacted stone and gravel layer will prevent subsequent movement that can cause tiles to crack. Otherwise the weight and volume of materials required may be outside the weight-bearing ability of the construction.

also use weed-suppressant mat directly under gravel, or under the hardcore itself.

A series of single paving slabs create an informal Japanese-style path that is easy to traverse and sympathetic in appearance. Lay slabs individually on the second layer of medium-grade gravel and infill with the finishing material. Over a small area, fine gravel can be used instead of jointing to infill between slabs loose laid over sand. This non-permanent technique provides flexibility and has a softer appearance.

Above: *Wooden slatted screens divide up the roof garden to create separate zones.*

WALLS AND SCREENS FOR OUTDOOR ROOMS

From trellis to painted walls and fenced boundaries to fabric screens, the partitions in your patio will define its style. For an outdoor room with an interior style, these choices are especially pertinent. You have the flexibility to use colours and textures and plants in the same way as you might for a room in your home.

Using Trellis

Trellis provides a quick and ready-made screening device for the outdoor room. A useful technique for any patio, it can create a decorative backdrop, a private area, or hide an unwanted view (see also using trellis for a classic backdrop on page 16 and for a flower-filled Mediterranean screen on page 40).

To customize it to the outdoor room, you can vary its appearance by tinting it in exterior-quality paint. Choose from colours such as restrained greys and putty tones, or for a more vibrant effect, brilliant blues set off foliage and flowers to perfection.

You can fix trellis panels directly to a plain wall or fence to create an interesting relief design. Alternatively, use the panels to create freestanding screens supported on timber posts (see opposite). In this situation, they make a perfect vehicle for twining plants, such as honeysuckle and jasmine, both of which give a long display of highly perfumed flowers. Augment these plants with combinations of climbing roses and clematis to take the season through from early summer to autumn.

Where there is no natural planting medium, a long trough can be furnished with a trellis screen. Troughs can be found in materials such as painted or natural wood, lightweight resin or modern zinc, all perfect for roof terraces where weight needs to be kept to a minimum. Troughs with attached screen panels can be fitted with castors to create movable room dividers.

Above: *Diamond-pattern mesh panels are fixed to a very solid timber framework, making a semi-opaque screen wall filled with a collection of terracotta pots.*

Creating Partitions

Newly constructed walls open up new structural opportunities. In the example on the left, a freestanding screen wall provides a complete separation from the garden, and gives a clean background against which to set the furniture. The wall is tied in with scaffolding poles, an inexpensive device that serves as structural support, leaving open sides for the view and a roof structure to support the sliding fabric sun canopy. Both the closed and open walls are fitted with long planting boxes and larger planters have been built at ground level.

Left: *A self-contained outdoor room constructed with scaffolding poles and a solid screen wall.*

ERECTING A TRELLIS SCREEN

Trellis is a versatile screening material that works well in a number of different settings. In outdoor rooms, free-standing panels can create a sense of privacy and seclusion around dining or seating areas. Since the panels let in light they are superior to solid walls or fencing when creating room-like divides in small areas. You can also add extra 'windows' using specially shaped panels available from upmarket trellis and treillage suppliers. These framed apertures can be square, arched or circular to suit different design themes.

1 Dig a hole 60cm (2ft) deep and around 23cm (9in) across to accommodate the first fence post together with a quantity of quick-set ready-mixed concrete. If you have several post holes to dig, it is worth hiring a special post hole digging tool to excavate the soil.

2 Position the post so that it is perfectly upright. Use a spirit level on two sides to check this and adjust its angle accordingly. If you are working on your own, loosely nail pieces of wood to keep the post in place. Check the post is perpendicular after attaching the wooden struts.

3 Preferably with someone holding the post, pour in the gravel, sand and cement mix (you can buy this pre-packaged for setting fence posts). Ram the mixture into the hole so that it is well packed around the post. Wait until the posts are solid before removing the supports.

4 Using the panel as a guide, dig the second posthole. As an alternative to digging postholes, and if the ground is not too stony, consider using spiked metal sockets that you drive into the ground using a special tool.

5 Once the concrete has set, hammer in a number of galvanized nails at an angle to attach the trellis panel firmly to the post. Use bricks to raise the panel off the ground and hold it at the correct height while you work.

6 Continue to build up the screen to the required size. Paint the trellis panels with an exterior-quality wood preservative or a decorative paint or stain. Protect any adjacent paving with plastic sheeting or newspapers.

Walls of Colour

A walled patio offers innumerable decorative possibilities, but there is always the risk of it running riot in such a restricted area. A plain cement-rendered wall cries out for a colour treatment, the tone of which will completely alter the mood of your space. Think of Marrakech and Yves St Laurent's famous Majorelle gardens, the intense blue of which is impossible to forget, and the towering, shocking-pink walls favoured by Mexican architects. These intense colours enable you to create a tropical paradise by providing a background bold enough to display the powerful forms of exotic foliage and flowers.

Strong earth tones, reminiscent of southern desert landscapes, will move the mood towards Santa Fe, with its classic Adobe architecture. Walls of ochre and burnt umber, while still dramatic in effect, offer a warm, relaxing atmosphere. These tones provide a strong visual support to arrangements of bold plant forms, including yucca and the phoenix palm, suggestive of hot, dry climates.

Walls do not have to make a major colour statement in themselves; they can rely instead on texture and relief

Above: *A bold shade of blue on the walls of the Majorelle Gardens in Marrakech.*

for effect. A neutral background of greys and creams makes for a subtle decoration suited to both classical and contemporary environments. Colour can be introduced by painting the wall with masonry paint, which you will need to reapply periodically. Alternatively, the cement mix can be tinted with a pigment, which produces a permanent, low-maintenance solution.

Additional Details

A plain, solid wall can create an overwhelming visual statement, and can benefit from some form of design additions and decorative detail to break it up. Wall plaques made from stone or terracotta, for example, make interesting relief details, while niches to display a figurative bust or statue can be carved into the structure. Freestanding plinths and columns make elegant platforms for sculptures or specimen plants, or a group in varying heights might make supports for an interesting arrangement for jardinières.

Left: *Hot planting with squares of coloured Perspex creates a counterpoint to the red wall.*

Above: *An open-air fireplace creates a cosy ambiance for late summer evenings.*

Openings in the structure itself will reduce its mass and provide peepholes through to the space beyond. Where privacy is not an issue, a fixed, glazed opening will admit light, provide a view and a weather barrier. Alternatively, wooden shutters would frame and focus the opening, and allow you to close it off for seclusion and protection.

Fencing Options

If you do not have a ready-made walled patio, you will have to enclose the boundary with fencing. Basic off-the-peg woven fencing panels are an inexpensive solution, but are neither uplifting nor durable. You can create your own designs, choosing from a range of screening options that are available by the roll. These include split bamboo and woven heather mixes that can be fixed to timber posts. Set these in concrete foundations or use special metal post-holding spikes designed for the purpose that can be used for a speedy solution where ground conditions permit. Ready-made panels made from reeds bordered by wooden frames provide an elegant, yet informal wall, while woven willow

is excellent for a country-style backdrop. You can make your own cool, Japanese-inspired screens by using string to tie bamboo poles into combinations of diagonals and verticals (see method on page 109). For a contemporary fence or screen, use narrow timber slats set in horizontal or vertical parallels. These can be made less solid by leaving small gaps between the slats, or set them in a double layer to provide complete privacy.

Fabric Panels and Screens

To make the most of the precious summertime, temporary screening devices can transform your outdoor room into an intimate entertaining space. Panels of fabric provide an easy way to create such effects. Fix them vertically on a wooden or metal framework, using cable or strong cord laced through eyelets, to provide an intimate enclosure. To create shade and privacy from above, fix sections of fabric horizontally on wires across a pergola. They can be drawn back concertina-fashion along wires strung between the cross members.

Fabric is lightweight, easy to install and can be opened and closed to accommodate different requirements. Suitable materials include traditional canvas and some of the many new high-tech synthetics that repel moisture and are easy to clean and maintain. These are suitable for relatively rigid installations as long as they are able to withstand breezy conditions. The fabric will act as a sail, however, placing extra strain on the supporting framework. Where a softer effect is required, consider curtains of floaty muslin.

Vertically fixed Roman blinds, drawn up into flat folds when open, are a versatile screening device. Classical striped ticking is a good fabric choice and might suggest a shady courtyard in southern France. The blinds can be easily attached to the crossbeam of a pergola fixed to the house wall, or construct a temporary freestanding framework just for the summer made from rustic timbers. These will need to be fixed firmly to withstand wind and weather.

Where it is not possible to create a structure, an off-the-peg dining gazebo might suit the purpose. These tented structures are supplied with curtains, which can be drawn against sun or light showers, and they can be fitted with light strings for tying back. Easily assembled, they can be folded up and stored.

PLANTS AND CONTAINERS FOR OUTDOOR ROOMS

The style of the outdoor room will dictate the containers and planting. A highly focussed garden space linking directly with the house, it needs a sense of co-ordination and will be most successful if the outdoor theme reflects the texture and ambiance of the interior, producing a comfortable visual transition between the two areas.

Above: *Hanging baskets create long-lasting confections of flowers and foliage.*

Left: *A Victorian-style conservatory leads on to a terrace. Period-style wirework and cast-iron containers complement the planting.*

Classic Approaches

A traditional theme gives the scope to introduce some rococo styling, with elaborate pedestal vases and urns made from cast iron and lead, or moulded from terracotta. These pieces are frequently decorated with a confection of cherubs and ribboned swags, or embossed relief fruit and flowers. They tend to be weighty, so can present problems for roof gardens and areas with reduced access. In such cases, use good quality replicas moulded from resin and glass-reinforced plastic (GRP).

Turn-of-the-century-style wirework offers another lightweight solution to support plants. The delicate interwoven system of fine wires translates well into elegant plant stands and étagères, its openwork structure suited to display a collection of pots. They can also be lined with sphagnum moss and plastic to disguise and contain the soil for direct planting.

For a romantic planting style use traditional containers filled with colourful flowers that can be changed throughout the year. Seasonal bedding plants create big splashes of instant colour in an outdoor room. Tender geraniums (*Pelargoniums*), love full sun and are the best container plants for giving endless summer colour with

minimal watering and maintenance. Bushy zonal types in blowsy pinks and vibrant reds make a great display in large containers, while elegant trailing ivy-leaf varieties with sophisticated deep magenta blooms, show off their graceful, trailing habit in tall urns and vases. Petunias love the sun too, and their blue, pink or purple blooms combine well with the trailing silvery foliage of *Helichrysum*. For those frequent shady spots, gleaming busy Lizzie, (*Impatiens*) cannot be surpassed for a continuous show of brilliant colour.

Modern Options

A contemporary outdoor room calls for a bolder, more structured approach. Clean-shaped planters with no superfluous ornamentation make sculptural statements that are especially effective when placed in oversized pairs or lined up in sequential, identical groups. Tall and relatively narrow forms make a huge impact and can be found in either soft round or robust, square-sectioned shapes. These combine most effectively with architectural shrubs, especially evergreens such as box, clipped in low shapes. These can be round or cubed, to counterbalance the container height and emphasize the sculptural effect. This creates a cool and understated European look, especially when the planters are made in the new, black, taupe or cream coloured terracotta.

Spiky or exotic plants also work well in a modern setting, offering a contrasting energetic style. Large architectural specimens, such as agave and yucca, fit the bill perfectly, as do palms and banana. However, these plants tend to be wide and sometimes top heavy so they need appropriately broad containers with enough physical weight and volume to sustain such vigorous giants.

Flowers are not out of place in a modern setting, but in order to complement the formal architecture, they should be applied in a structured way. Plant bold, simple flowers in blocks or groups, keeping to a single co-ordinated colour tone or shape. Canna lilies offer bold, exotic form with striking foliage and vibrant blooms in shades of orange, yellow and red. More discreetly, the tall, slender green stems of agapanthus are surmounted by clusters of blue or white bell-shaped blooms and are divinely cool and elegant.

Flowers for Colour

Pelargoniums, also known as geraniums, love full sun and are the best container plants for endless vibrant colour, minimal watering and low maintenance. Bushy forms in blowsy pinks and reds give a brilliant display in large containers. Elegant, ivy-leafed forms, available in sophisticated deep reds and magentas, show off their graceful, trailing habit in tall vases and urns. For overflowing, continental-style window boxes, choose bright red or pink balcony forms. Some, such as *P. crispum*, suit a topiary treatment.

Endless attractive combinations can also be made with petunias, in lovely shades of pale to deepest blue. For shady spots, scarlet, orange and pink busy Lizzy (*Impatiens*), give an iridescent show. For a country look, mix bright-yellow marigolds (*Tagetes*) and orange nasturtiums (*Tropaeolum majus*), with blue *Felicia* or *Brachyscome*.

Above: *A massed display of pots with mono-planting makes a stunning wall feature. Geranium is really the only choice for this treatment because of its low water requirements.*

PLANTING A WALL BASKET

A bare wall can seem an inhospitable place for growing flowers, but a large manger-style basket or a hayrack, up to twice the size of the container illustrated, has enough space for a substantial amount of compost (soil mix) and a good variety of plants, including smaller evergreen shrubs and spring bulbs. Group several baskets together for additional impact. These are useful where there are no borders for growing climbers and wall shrubs in the ground. Long trailing plants, including Surfinia petunias for summer and ivies for winter, cover bare wall effectively.

1 Using handfuls of sphagnum moss (collected from a sustainable source), begin to line the basket to produce a 'nest' capable of holding the plants and compost (soil mix). Alternatively, line the back section with polythene.

2 Put a little compost into the bottom of the basket to support the plants' root-balls (roots). Make holes in the moss and feed the plants through from the front so that the neck of each one lies within the basket, surrounded by a moss collar.

3 Continue to build up the front of the basket. Then add some larger basket plants in the top, such as the variegated fuchsia and ivy-leaved geranium shown here. Fill in the gaps with more compost and water well.

Left: *A pale grey palette makes this tiny space feel larger. The subtle silver/ grey and white planting maintains the cool, airy feel.*

Sensory Planting

Warm, summer evenings suggest lazy salads and barbecues, so think about including containers of aromatic herbs to add flavour and colour to your dishes. Rosemary and thyme flavour roast meats, while pungent fennel seeds and stalks add a special touch to fish. Don't forget parsley, coriander, marjoram and tarragon.

Still, evening warmth releases flower perfumes, bringing a sense of night-time romance to your patio. Especially effective are annual white tobacco plants (*Nicotiana affinis*) and night-scented stocks (*Matthiola incana*) that pervade the evening air with their musky scent. The glossy-leaved, evergreen shrubs Japanese mock orange (*Pittosporum tobira*) and Mexican orange blossom (*Choisya ternata*) reward year after year with their sweet, citrus-like scent. Lilies (*Lilium*) have a glamour to match their perfume, while lavish, but

Right: *Blue plumbago makes a perfect foil for the intense, ultra-sky-blue wall.*

Far right: *The heavy, drooping blooms of the datura (Brugmansia) creates interior theatre.*

poisonous, datura (*Brugmansia*) waits until dusk before releasing its fragrance, attracting night-time pollinators to its huge dangling bells. Pots of equally tender gardenia and stephanotis will enrich your table setting with their evocative scents.

Planting for Height

Climbing plants enhance the vertical dimension of your boundary walls, arbours and pergolas, and some can have the

added bonus of fragrance. Common jasmine (*Jasminum officinale*) and the valuable star jasmine (*Trachelospermum jasminoides*), one of the few flowering evergreen climbers, have a rich, oriental-style perfume. For a more European touch, sweetly scented roses, such as 'Alberic Barbier' and 'Madame Alfred Carriere', give out an evocative, old-fashioned fragrance. All of these flowers are white, so they will glow at night in any reflected light, while infusing the air with their fragrance, which is especially intense in the evening.

Climbers with coloured flowers make their impact in daylight. *Passiflora* 'Amethyst', the purple passion flower, is a must for a sheltered spot, while also loving a sunny wall, the classic blue *P. caerulea* will finish with showy orange fruits in late summer. To fill in spaces, clematis will integrate with other climbers, mingling especially well with climbing roses to increase the length of the flowering season. They can stand alone, trained on

tripods to make local features, or be allowed to cover an area of trellis. Unbeatable scramblers for hot climates are showy bougainvilleas in irrepressible shades of orange, red and purple, the power of which can be beautifully offset by soft, powdery blue plumbago.

Integrating Containers

In the outdoor room, containers fulfil some important functions, enabling you to introduce focal points and to alter and emphasize the planting design according to seasonal requirements. The pots themselves make a huge architectural contribution to the design, so choose with care to ensure that you are sending out the right message in terms of material, colour and shape. Generally, the most successful way to arrange containers is to select those that match in either material or shape.

Below: *Three tall square shaped containers planted with tightly clipped box make a strong sculptural statement.*

In this way, you can build up groups of containers to make strong visual statements.

You may already have a collection of interior plants, in which case you could repeat either the form or colour of their pots in the garden design. Oriental stoneware pots exist both in sensuously curvaceous forms and tall, straight-sided designs that can complement the inside/outside function excellently. Such examples can be found in earthy, wood-fired finishes that would work well within a restrained contemporary design. They also exist in a subtle range of dreamy glazes, ranging from celadon green through to deep blues and purples. Such glazes can introduce smouldering elements of colour to your outdoor room. These are usually frost resistant, which means the same containers can be used indoors and out, giving a consistent element.

Ceramic and terracotta are more porous than stoneware and the clay body has an effect on the depth of the glaze that can be achieved. These pots can often be found in brilliantly coloured glazes, including yellows, reds, greens and blues, which contribute well to a design with a hotter theme. However, be aware that these glazes are often fragile and vulnerable to water penetration, and this will lead to frost damage in cold climates. Always check that pots are suitable for outdoor use before making a purchase, or be sure to empty them of soil in winter and preferably store them somewhere dry and frost-free.

STRUCTURES AND FURNITURE FOR OUTDOOR ROOMS

Structures and furniture for outdoor living include pergolas and awnings to create shade, and luxurious seating areas in which to relax and entertain. You might like a modern streamlined barbecue to prepare food, or perhaps a rustic style with a fire pit. Other ideas for an enviable outdoor space are a plunge pool, jacuzzi or shower.

Above: *Soak up the atmosphere of an open-air barbecue on a summer's evening.*

Constructions in Wood

Wood is a material that gives permanence and stability to the outdoor room and timber is easy to source and work. So use traditional wooden garden structures, such as pergolas, shelving and seating, and also create or commission new structures in wood to give your outdoor space the permanent character of a room. Bold sections make ideal posts, with strength and the ability to blend with different roof structures and styles. Narrow wooden slats provide an elegant, lightweight canopy that can be angled like a pitched roof. Another option is yacht wires strung through the beams to support a temporary fabric awning for shade and style.

An Overhanging Roof

A solid, overhanging roof gives you a veranda suitable for all-weather use. The roof structure might be clad in tiles or slates, providing excellent shade, something that is crucial in hotter climates. In more temperate regions, where sunlight is at more of a premium, transparency is desirable. In this case, the roof can be broken up with sections of glass or Perspex while still providing protection from bad weather.

Barbecues and Dining

The pergola can be interpreted in a freestanding form to create a special feature area for a barbecue and dining space. You might think of enclosing two sides with walls to increase the intimacy and provide shelter. The walls would provide a support and chimney for the barbecue and make it possible to include a preparation area. The barbecue, combined with an open fire and comfy sofas, will tempt you outside even in the cooler evenings.

This design would be suitable to accommodate a proper outdoor kitchen, complete with power and plumbing for preparation, refrigerator and cooking. Having it all to hand in this way adds an extra dimension to your daily life. If your culinary ambitions extend to it, try using an outdoor pizza or bread oven. The pergola shelter can be used in all seasons, if the weather is not too severe.

Above: *Tiny spaces need vertical thinking. A planted wall, a water feature, hidden cupboards and bike storage leave room for a sheltered canopy and a cantilevered bench.*

Above: *A screen wall and canopy provide stylish protection for an outdoor kitchen.*

Heat and flame are compelling elements, and a fire pit makes a wonderful focal point for a social gathering at night. This simple and innovative concept is basically just a hole in the ground where you can burn logs or coal. It could be used for warmth or be readily adapted for cooking for small or large numbers. A fire pit might be built into an area of terracing that has been designed with low-level seating and an informal dining space. This is an excellent project for a keen home-improvement enthusiast, as it is simple to construct using brick or rendered cement blocks. Stand-alone fire grates that come in a very wide range of stylish designs are now readily available as alternatives.

All-purpose Furniture

An outdoor dining room needs practical furniture. The decision about style depends on your taste and preferences, but what the furniture is made out of and how it is made are crucial if it is to withstand the rigours of sun, rain and varying temperatures.

A generous-sized table is a must and it needs to feel solid and stable. The refectory-style provides a good-looking timber option, using bench seating that echoes the table's uncomplicated lines. Benches are easy and informal, adapting to suit the number of guests. The simple, clean, everyday look can easily be livened up with coordinating fabrics for the seat cushions and table cover.

Contemporary outdoor furniture designs often combine wood and metal to create elegant and streamlined tables and chairs that are streets away in style from clumsy, conventional shapes. These provide a manageable, lighter-weight option that blends well in either a modern or a more traditional setting.

Above: *Screen walls with closable shutters and a timber-slatted roof admit light but ensure protection from damp and breezes.*

Modern-day furniture needs to be adaptable to cope with a faster lifestyle. Large parties and unexpected guests demand tables that are adaptable in size. Many designs are supplied with sections you can slot in to extend the length, but two square tables may suit you better. These can be set around the garden for small groups and then brought together as required to accommodate larger numbers. To really enjoy a long relaxed meal, the dining chair should be comfortable. Cushions are a must, though some seats are made of soft, synthetic fabrics that do the same job. It helps if chairs are light enough to move around easily, and for winter storage you might consider designs that can be folded or stacked.

Comfortable, weather-resistant outdoor furniture is now widely available. New plastics technology has produced fibres that can be woven into basket chairs with all the charm of wicker but with zippy, modern styling. These seem to have been created with just the outdoor sitting room in mind. Comfy sofas team up with generous armchairs and low-slung tables designed for after-dinner conversation. When you want to snuggle up with a book and escape, choose a sinuous day bed or, even more eye-catching, a huge, circular lounging pad enclosed beneath a curvaceous woven cover. Natural colours, such as sand, coffee and cream, create a sophisticated look that works beautifully within the indoor/outdoor space.

Soft Furnishings

With space always at a premium, it is good to have a few enormous floor cushions that can be stacked away when not needed. They are available covered in brilliantly coloured weather-resistant fabrics, some plain and some screen printed in super-sized flower and foliage designs. Matching deckchairs and a parasol will complete a tropical garden set. To complete the integration of interior and exterior, try a colour theme using other soft furnishings.

Above: *Resin fibre imitating cane is shaped into inviting, organically styled chairs that make a crisp, sculptural statement.*

Below left: *Floor cushions and a low granite table create a stylish spot to eat sushi.*

Below: *Cushions and a mattress transform a low oriental table into a superb sun bed.*

A pavilion would make an excellent setting for passing a lazy afternoon. Many designs are available, often from wrought iron, which will look attractive and create a focal point all year around.

Below: *A hot tub is simple to install, with decking giving cover for the feed pipes.*

Left: *An outdoor shower in an available corner of a tiny roof terrace will freshen you up on a hot day.*

In summer, furnish the pavilion with a fitted canopy and curtains to screen out the sun. Pile floor cushions, Eastern style, over the ground and you have an instant Bedouin tent.

Patio Bathing

Outdoor bathing is now an attainable luxury. At its simplest, a small plunge pool gives you the chance to cool off on a hot day. It can be built as an 'above-ground' feature if you intend to conceal it within a stepped deck arrangement, and so will not need expensive excavation. If you prefer warmth, a Jacuzzi or hot tub could be incorporated into a patio. A long, narrow lap pool is a real luxury for keen swimmers and it makes an elegant feature. Advanced pool technology makes real exercise possible, even in a restricted space – powerful jets set into one wall push water out with such force that you swim against a real current.

A quiet, shady place provides respite from the sun when it's time to cool off. A built structure is not always the most desirable option, especially when a feeling of space

Above: *Simplicity and contemporary sculptural form – this sleek sun bed is the perfect place to relax.*

and movement is wanted. Yachting sails combine naturally with water and air, and this marine technology has been adopted for the land. The latest shade canopies incorporate the sail principle, stretching hi-tech textiles into elegant, almost bird-like forms that seem to float between their tensioned supports. These make a beautiful design statement in an outdoor space. They can be sited beside a pool to shelter a seating area, arranged to form a link between the interior and exterior space or to create a niche for bathing.

An outdoor shower is an invigorating way to start or end the day. Find a corner close to the house in which to set up a small showering area. Make a screen wall to hide the plumbing and fix up one or more showerheads. Provide a soakaway for the used water with a slatted plinth to cover it. Towels and soaps can be stored informally in baskets placed on a long, low bench seat. If possible, site the shower where you have direct access to it from the bathroom or your bedroom for an even more luxurious bath-time treat.

ORNAMENT FOR OUTDOOR ROOMS

The outdoor room provides an ideal setting through which to exhibit ornamental and architectural features, providing both a garden stage and backdrop. However, as the space is likely to be used for a range of different purposes, the level and type of display and decoration should be adaptable in order to cope with these varying demands.

Above: *Animal sculptures like this wire-mesh chicken bring fun to a patio.*

Above: *The organic form of these tall bar stools with curving metal legs shows modern furniture as a sculptural statement.*

Style Continuity

In a defined space like an outdoor room, it is important to maintain a clear impression of its style. Space is at a premium so it is preferable to keep ornamentation to a minimum, perhaps using it as part of overall decoration rather than adding too many set pieces. Work in a small palette of colours to reduce an impression of clutter, and focus your approach towards the texture of materials. Picking up and repeating some of the design elements of the interior will help the sense of continuity between inside and out. Pale background colours such as soft greys and creams give an added impression of space, permitting ornamental elements to be shown off clearly.

Useful and Ornamental

Furnishings offer decorative possibilities in their own right – they are also likely to take up a significant amount of space. Care in the selection of furnishings will ensure that they play an integral role in the overall design concept.

Chairs, especially in modern designs, offer plenty of ornamental potential. New plastics and moulding processes permit sculptural forms that introduce their own decorative statement. The tall bar stools shown to the left demonstrate some of the possibilities. With their organic form, the metal legs seem to have grown just like stems, with the seat appearing like an opening flower bud or a bursting seed pod.

Garden planters, too, can make decorative statements. The traditional Mediterranean olive jar in curvaceous 'Ali Baba' shapes can be found in giant sizes that really make a visual splash. Made from terracotta, their soft colour and texture evoke a sun-filled climate and will add a touch of southern warmth to the garden.

Sculptural Form

Using sculpture in the landscape is a technique that allows the display of contemporary artworks, commercially produced objects or interesting 'found' objects. The use of such objects continues the interior décor theme.

Contemporary sculptures, often abstract in form, can be curvaceous, inspired by a human or animal shape. Alternatively, strictly angular and geometric shapes might fit more appropriately into a cool, architectural concept.

The physical presence of practical features often assumes a defining ornamental role. For example, the shape of a shade can add to the overall visual value of the space. A screen wall will physically anchor the canopy, but also visually, by use of the same colour paint. The large organic ornament on the opposite page could be overpowering, but it is coordinated by the colour finish.

Wall Decorations

Exterior walls can be enlivened by the inclusion of decorative objects, and don't use up valuable floor space. Salvaged household items can also be given a makeover and found a new life on a wall or screen. An ornamental door, an old gate or iron

Above: *A group of identical earthenware oil jars makes a strong sculptural statement.*

Above: *In this dramatic space, tall timber pillars and a triptych of narrow wall prints lead the way to a sphere and sculptural roof.*

railings can be transformed by a coat of paint and make an effective *trompe l'oeil* effect. More conventionally, use carved or moulded plaques, which make excellent details and are easy to fix on the surface, or can be incorporated into openings in the wall's structure.

Grouping Similar Pieces

Collections of similar items work well where space allows. A group of old wirework jardinières would add interest to a traditional terrace. Striking pots and vases make a big impact when arranged as a highlight feature.

Right: *A redundant Victorian fireplace sees a new role as part of a planting design to decorate a boundary wall.*

WATER FEATURES FOR OUTDOOR ROOMS

The possibilities for water features are many, dividing between the natural or formal (in style) and the functional or decorative (in purpose). For an outdoor room, formality and functionality make a good combination, so opt for water sources for bathing and cooking, or features that accentuate the architecture.

Above: *Enliven a tiny formal pool with a quirky fountain such as this.*

Water to Delight the Senses

The presence of water adds life to an outdoor room, encouraging wildlife visitors, such as birds, butterflies and frogs. Water, which sparkles in sunlight and reflects shadows and shapes, can be organized in a diversity of forms, from an energetic gurgling fall to a still, shallow reflective pool in which birds can splash and bathe.

A formal water feature, due to its organized structure and appearance, is more likely to complement the outdoor room. A modestly sized pool with enough space to allow people to move around it makes an eye-catching centrepiece for a formal garden. It can be constructed above ground by means of a retaining wall of rendered blockwork, brick or stone. Alternatively, it can be dug out and finished with an edging at ground level. Either type of construction requires a waterproof lining and a means of filtering the water to keep it clean and aerated.

A round pool is a classic design feature, and seems to work well in the above-ground format. It is always pleasant to gaze into water and this style allows the addition of a broad seating ledge to replace the coping. A ground-level pool has the advantage of being viewed from above. It can be set into a wooden deck or incorporated into a paved terrace or courtyard floor. Irregular shapes can be integrated into an existing architectural structure to enhance the features of a background wall. Alternatively, a rectangular form, bounded by benches, provides a peaceful retreat.

The effect of still, dark water is calming and tranquil, aspects you can accentuate by introducing water lilies. A narrow canal of shallow water can bring a different dimension to the garden room and an interesting way to divide space. You may even be able to incorporate a path of stepping-stones in a rectangular pool to help dissect the space.

Moving Water

An integral fountain creates movement and sound and a sense of life and energy in either a raised or ground-level pool. Various visual effects are possible depending on the pump and water outlet. A single, central spray, for example, will give the classical romantic style of fine, cascading droplets. More modern jets can be arranged singly or in groups to gurgle high or low to break the surface tension.

A cascade effect can be readily incorporated into a rectangular pool by means of an integrated fountain wall of water. It can take the form of a free-standing screen, or it can be built into an existing supporting wall. The pump can be set so that water emerges in a rush from a mouth or chute, or it can trickle gently over a wide ledge. A selection of ready-made fountains in stainless steel are a simple solution to introduce some elements of gleam and sparkle.

Right: *This glazed timber bathing cabin is the ultimate private space, overlooking a series of formal pools in a jungle of planting.*

Right: *An above-ground plunge pool can be easily incorporated into a timber deck.*

Tailor the aural qualities of water to your requirements. Many water features produce a variety of sounds, some soothing, others energetic. When selecting effects for a small garden space, consider their proximity to your neighbours – they may not appreciate the noise escaping into their space. On the other hand, the sound of a gentle cascade or fast-moving waterfall breaking over stones can be used effectively to disguise urban noise.

Water Containers

Any watertight, frostproof container is suitable for creating a small water feature and is ideal for areas of raised deck or on roof terraces, where a more traditional pond may be impractical. There are many options, from grey steel bowls in geometric shapes to wide shallow stone or concrete bowls. Wooden barrels, available from most garden centres, are good water containers and come ready-treated against rot. Alternatively, free-standing stone fonts or troughs, large terracotta bowls or curvaceous urns make instant gardens for miniature water lilies. Large bowls or pots, which can be bought with a pre-drilled drainage hole, can incorporate a small fountain, whereby the pump sits on a level spot at the bottom with its plastic-coated wire passing through the hole, which is then sealed with silicon. Most small pumps are designed to run off mains electricity. Plants added to the water in barrels or bowls are best kept in baskets to control their growth and for easier maintenance, and it is best to use rain water in any small planted water feature. Avoid placing container water gardens in a hot spot.

Safety note: *Children should be supervised at all times when near water. Protective fences can deter toddlers, but if children use your patio space, the safest measure is to avoid water features.*

Above: *A cascade of water falls from a concrete spout into the pebbled pool below.*

Above: *The constant trickle of water provides movement and gentle sound.*

Above: *This steel water container can house aquatic and moisture-loving plants.*

LIGHTING FOR OUTDOOR ROOMS

Outdoor lighting for the patio has to be decorative and practical. Avoid the prison-yard effect produced by overlighting, as this will destroy any sense of intimacy. The lighting you choose for your outdoor room will depend on its function. A contemporary jacuzzi and deck area needs a very different treatment compared with an elegant period-style dining space.

Above: *Simple lights with paper shades are perfect for special celebrations.*

Basic Lighting

Once you have sorted out basic safety lighting for steps and other changes in level (see page 149), and have adequate illumination around any cooking areas, you can begin to light your outdoor space more creatively. Courtyards used as outdoor rooms have much the same lighting considerations as indoor rooms.

For a start, remove any wall-mounted, downward-facing floodlights, as these have more to do with security than creating a relaxing ambiance. In addition, avoid generating unnecessary light pollution by installing too many lights – this is likely to alienate neighbours as well as obliterate any view of the stars. Keep additional

Above: *Interior backlighting provides a distinctive atmosphere at this stylish home, adding shadows and glinting reflections around the deep black pool.*

Above: *Mini floods set into the paving softly illuminate the walls.*

lighting at a relatively low level, mimicking indoor lamps set on occasional tables, or use contemporary wall lights to throw the beam upwards. Even modern outdoor fairy lights can make a useful contribution.

Spa Lighting

Consider fitting white or coloured optical-fibre lighting around a hot tub set into a deck area. Each light strand in a large bundle is accommodated in a hole drilled through the wood and so this is something that is far easier to do during the final stages of deck construction. Discrete neon-blue LED (light-emitting diode) spots can also be set into decking to produce random scatterings of

light, to define the shape of the tub or be set out in rows to highlight and define steps.

The lighting for an outdoor bathroom needs to create a relaxing atmosphere. Spa baths often come with their own integral lighting and so the surrounding area can be softly lit – perhaps by candles or spherical ceramic oil lamps.

Try uplighting surrounding specimen plants or an interestingly shaped tree to create an oasis effect or throw the focus on to a sculpture or water feature that can be viewed from the hot tub.

Dining by Starlight

In colder climates, opportunities for alfresco dining are limited, so make the most of those precious warm, dry evenings. In a period setting, candlesticks and candelabras with a distressed, gothic finish add a grandiose touch. Wind some ivy trails around the uprights and set church candles in clear glass holders among low-level flower and foliage arrangements. If the table is underneath a pergola, consider winding LED fairy lights through the climbers (see method below) and hang coloured glass tea-light lanterns at varying heights. You can also weave LED fairy lights through the trellis screens surrounding a dining area to create a more intimate atmosphere.

Left: *Ornate glass lanterns, an array of tea lights and chunky church candles add a softly glowing touch of romance to this outdoor dining area.*

INSTALLING FAIRY LIGHTS

Modern outdoor LED fairy or string lights come in a range of colours and are more luminous and durable than those fitted with standard bulbs. Use them to add a bit of magic to an outdoor dining room at night. They can be easily and securely attached to structures such as trellis panels, but also try weaving them through climbers on a pergola, over a small specimen tree or topiary standard stem or, for a contemporary effect, up through the vertical culms of bamboo. Wind them more tightly to concentrate the intensity of the lights.

1 Wind the lights around the supports, maintaining an even, but unordered, coverage of LEDs. It is much easier to do this if you bunch the cable up and feed it out. Check distribution by temporarily plugging it in to an extension lead.

2 To keep the LEDs firmly in their correct positions, use plastic-coated wires or small black cable ties. If you are fixing lights to plant stems, use soft twine rather than wire, which will cut into the plant stems over time.

3 The transformer needs a waterproof housing if it is positioned outdoors. Use a qualified electrician if you need to install a new socket. Feed the thin cable through from outdoors and plug it into the transformer.

THE EDIBLE GARDEN

The challenge of creating a patio in which you can cultivate seasonal produce – fresh fruit, vegetables, herbs, edible flowers and blooms for cutting – is a question of harnessing space efficiently. Your growing area may be restricted to a small terrace, but with clever planning and the careful selection of produce to fit with your location, a courtyard or patio can overflow with fresh, home-grown delights.

All kinds of edibles can be grown in large pots, troughs and even hanging baskets, or in easy-to-construct raised beds. Practicality is essential in the kitchen garden, with flooring that allows all-weather access. As well as growing crops, incorporating more decorative planting in the form of herbs, flowers, shrubs and climbers draws in pollinating and beneficial insects (natural predators) as well as keeping the patio looking pretty.

Left: *Raised planting beds allow you to grow produce all year round, even where there is no natural soil available. Create them with heavy timber planks and make an allowance for water to drain freely.*

FLOORING FOR THE EDIBLE GARDEN

A vegetable garden should be practical, with easy access for planting, maintenance and harvesting. This is especially true for a small patio space. Floors should be functional, paths should be wide enough for a wheelbarrow to pass and beds should be easy to reach for frequent tending, watering and harvesting.

Above: *Loose-laid paving slabs have an informal look, and provide a secure walkway.*

Gravel and Chippings

Ideal in a productive patio, gravel is easy to lay, inexpensive and allows water to soak away naturally. Normally it is sold as washed pea gravel for use in making concrete. You can buy it in large sacks from builders' merchants or have it delivered in bulk. Its slightly yellowish-grey tone blends in with most architectural backgrounds, so it has a universal application.

Lay gravel directly on to well compacted hardcore or crusher run. Bear in mind, however, that gravel has a tendency to move underfoot, so retain it with some sort of edging material. A terracotta or stone edging tile fits the purpose, while timber planks work well, too.

Gravel is ideal for paths between raised beds, as the walls of the beds work to retain both soil and gravel. Avoid laying it more than about

Above: *This gravel-surrounded plot benefits from a protective boundary of shrubs and trees to shelter the produce from cold winds.*

5cm (2in) thick or pushing a wheelbarrow becomes hard work. You can also lay it over a weed-suppressant mat to keep it tidy. Another approach is to mix the gravel with a little dry cement, and water it in gently to set and compact in place.

Slate chippings provide an equally informal, though more stylish, flooring treatment. The larger texture and soft grey tones give a more contemporary look and blend especially well with an exotic- or Mediterranean-style planting. It makes an excellent complement to silvery leafed herbs, such as santolina and lavender, and to vegetables, such as globe artichokes, aubergines (eggplants), black beans and tomatoes.

An informal pathway through the gravel will make your footing more secure and ease the task of pushing heavy wheelbarrows and cultivators.

Stepping-stones do the job perfectly and fit well with this type of garden. Set them in place on the surface of the ground and lay the gravel to fill in around them. Old, heavy pieces of reclaimed timber work very well in this situation, too, especially if it matches the material used for the walls of the raised beds.

Disguised Concrete

Concrete sleepers that look remarkably like weathered wood are available from builders' merchants and larger home-improvement stores. They come in easy-to-handle lengths and, laid within gravel, add a distinctive tone to the vegetable plot. Prepare the ground thoroughly before laying, using well-compacted

Above: *A gravel path works well in a productive garden such as this one.*

hardcore topped with sand, as unevenness or soil shifting can cause cracks to appear. Use them to create entire pathways, hard-wearing steps, centrepiece designs and edgings.

Paving Slabs

One of the most practical and hard-wearing surface materials for the productive garden is paving slabs. Unlike gravel and slate, which become weedy if you spill soil on to them, stone or concrete slabs or quarry tiles are easy to keep clean with a hose or brush, as well as weed free. A foundation of blobs of cement laid on hardcore and sand provides a durable base for any kind of paving and results in a smooth, level surface that is easy to maintain.

It may be that a relaxed look is more desirable, so you might want to lay tiles and slabs directly on to

Right: *Rectangular concrete blocks, created in timber moulds, set in a gravel pathway.*

the earth. Level and compact the earth first and then apply a good layer of sand to receive the pavers, which are tapped down to bed them in. Over time, the paving may become slightly uneven, but this only adds to the charm.

Above: *A gravel floor is a practical option, with zinc containers holding flowering pinks, scented geraniums, cabbages and thyme.*

Below: *Paving slabs bedded in a concrete base are secure and practical. Terracotta pots and kitchen herbs soften the look.*

Above: *Reclaimed setts are laid without mortar to allow water to run away.*

Above: *Rustic cobblestones make it easy to brush and hose off debris.*

Above: *Flagstones offer an attractive and sturdy floor for a produce-filled garden box.*

The Kitchen Garden

The potager, or kitchen garden, is a working area of the garden, so a stableyard styling could fit well with a patio theme. There are several ways to achieve this look using paving blocks. These have a distinctive look, being much thicker and with a smaller surface area than other paving materials.

Cobblestones or Setts

A traditional form of paving for stableyards and mews passageways, cobblestones for this purpose were selected for their round shape and high-domed profile, which sheds water and makes it easy to hose them down and brush them off.

Cobbles are normally set into cement mortar, with gaps between them to allow for water run-off. They are smooth and gleam beautifully when wet, but can be uncomfortable to walk on.

It may be possible to source cobbles from building reclamation yards, but it is more common today to use new pieces of granite known as setts. These are square in shape with a flat, low-slip profile. They are extremely dense and durable, and are perfectly suitable for a hard-working surface. It is normal to set them into a concrete base but you can also bed them into sand, enabling excess water to run away easily.

Good-value concrete flooring appears in many guises. Concrete setts are most realistic, while modular paving slabs, which are often used to make driveways, offer a variety of sizes, tones and textures suited to paving, steps and edgings.

Brickwork

Old brick paths can be seen in many Victorian and Edwardian walled kitchen gardens and if you're looking for a period feel for your productive patio, lay brick paths using one of the patterns below. Reclaimed frost-proof bricks are charming, but normal wall bricks tend to be soft and suitable only for light traffic. For a durable flooring use strong, hardwearing engineering bricks, made from dense clay fired at high temperatures to withstand water penetration and frost damage. Choose colours such as deep plum and nearly black for a modern look.

The way you arrange brick pavers will affect the look of the garden. Use a simple pattern or stretcher bond, such as that found in brick walls, for hard-working areas, traditional cottage-garden-style plots and pathways. The herringbone bond has a more ornamental feel – but cutting triangles of brick to fill in gaps along the margins is complicated. The basketweave pattern is modular and therefore useful if you are paving around square or rectangular beds, and looks best over larger areas.

  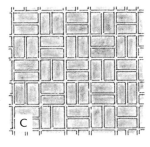

Above: *When laying brick pavers, you can use a simple pattern or stretcher bond (A), a herringbone bond (B) or a basketweave (C).*

Floor-level Planting

Hedging is a traditional way to edge beds for the kitchen garden and it combines well with brick paths – the scale of the brick sits comfortably with small edging plants.

For a more formal arrangement of vegetables and flowers, organize them into a parterre design. Create a framework of beds divided by paths edged with evergreens. Box is ideal; deep green and slow growing, it needs shaping only once or twice a year. Lavender and santolina have the added bonus of flowers and scent.

Take the idea a step further by creating a floor made up entirely of plants. Using the knot-garden format, make an intricate design using evergreen foliage set off by gravel. This centrepiece would be a perfect foil to exuberant vegetables and flowers and the potager would then always have an element of year-round interest.

Right: *In this parterre, the beds are edged with box. Red and green salad leaves form a geometric pattern beside yellow feverfew and orange marigolds.*

MAKING A PARTERRE

There are numerous pattern variations for knot gardens (with interweaving strands) and parterres (separate shapes and blocks). Even before the plants have knit together, the simple parterre shape illustrated appears sufficiently well defined to begin planting and sowing herbs and crops. Thorough ground preparation prior to planting the box edging, incorporating plentiful organic matter, promotes more rapid establishment.

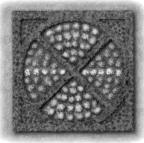

1 Use a set square to check the right angles making up the outer square. Create diagonals and, at the centre, fix a peg with a length of string attached to mark out a circle.

2 This simple pattern, which you can mark out on the ground with sand or white marker paint, is planted at 15–20cm (6–8in) intervals with dwarf box.

3 Within two years the box plants will have knitted together to make a seamless hedge. Trim them in late spring and again in late summer using hand shears.

4 Depending on the scale of your potager and your requirements, you can either plant each segment with just a single type of plant in a grid pattern or subdivide each one.

WALLS FOR THE EDIBLE GARDEN

Enclosures play many important roles in the kitchen garden. Not only do they give shelter from cold or damaging winds, they provide a support for training fruit trees and climbers and help to maintain a microclimate for your plants. Any existing wall should be employed as part of your design and new partitions, such as fencing, hurdles or hedging, can be added to suit the produce.

Above: *A south-facing brick wall is an ideal location for climbing gourds.*

Walls for Training Fruit

Masonry walls, built from brick, stone or blockwork, have heat-retaining properties that give them the edge over other screening choices. They provide an ideal situation to train more tender fruit bearers, such as cherry, peach and apricot, and in colder climates pears will benefit, too.

Depending on the specimen, choose between espalier-style plants, where side branches are trained horizontally from a central vertical stem, and fan-trained examples, where several stems are produced from the base of the plant and fanned out equally all around (see also page 45).

These training systems need wall support. The most practical and least obtrusive is to have a series of wires fixed horizontally, enabling plants to be tied in place as they grow. Strong galvanized wire can be fixed to vine eyes and tightened using a tensioning device. The closer to the horizontal the wires are, the more likely it is that flower buds will develop. For extra support, thread the wire through a sequence of eyes set at intervals of no more than 1.8m (6ft).

Above: *The side wall of a timber hut provides a sheltered seating corner and a support for the vine-covered pergola.*

Below: *The roots of the golden hop spread over any available wall or partition.*

WHERE TO GROW FRUIT

• On a south-facing wall – choose figs, peaches, apricots, grapes and pears. This site will be too hot for apples.
• On a west-facing wall – suitable for all fruits except those that require maximum sunshine and warmth. A good spot for cordon tomatoes, which like some shade from the midday sun.
• On an east-facing wall – this site only gets the morning sun, so tougher forms are needed here. Avoid anything where early blossom might get damaged by frost melting too rapidly in the morning sun. Grow fruit that won't flower early, such as raspberries.

• On a north-facing wall – this is the shadiest and coolest aspect, but options include the sour 'Morello' cherry, cooking apples and blackberries (although these won't be as sweet as they would be on a sunnier site).
• On trellis screens, archways and pergolas – anything with a strong climbing habit, such as squash, smaller fruited pumpkins and climbing courgettes, will benefit from getting light from two directions. Grapes and kiwis grow well on pergolas and arches. On trellis, try thornless blackberries and hybrid berries.

Right: *A deciduous hedge gives a sheltering screen around this vegetable garden.*

Multi-stranded, stainless-steel yachting wire is another option. This is stronger than galvanized wire, but it, and its fixings, are more expensive. Climbers and wall-trained shrubs are heavy, especially when laden with fruit, so make sure all bolts and eyes are of adequate size and length to be fixed securely to a wall (see also page 45).

Building New Walls

For a traditional walled kitchen you might want to replace existing fences or low walls with higher enclosing walls – if planning regulations permit. This creates more shade but will provide a sheltered microclimate. A traditional period walled garden would have used brick. A breeze (cinder) block wall will be much cheaper and can be built by an experienced amateur, but will need a coat of cement render applying

to give a clean finish to the wall. An element of colour will add interest – a tinted white is clean and bright, or a warmer ochre or terracotta hue will help to hold the heat of the sun. The render can be tinted with pigments to provide a permanent colour finish, or painted over regularly with a

masonry product to keep it fresh. A brick theme could also be introduced by building brick piers or topping the breeze-block wall with engineering bricks.

Below: *The cordon method of training employs heavily pruned single stems, tied diagonally to horizontal wires.*

Below: *The espalier method of training fruit is productive, decorative and a good method to use on a high, warm wall. All fruit trees can be trained in this way, popular varieties being apple, pear and plum.*

Above: *A flourishing runner bean uses a metal handrail to support its climbing, leafy tendrils.*

Left: *Off-the-peg trellis panels make instant plant trainers. These have been attached to the wall and painted in a pale colour so they disappear into the background.*

Trellis Support for Climbing Crops

Wooden latticework trellis provides an alternative means of training climbers. These ready-made panels are useful for a range of lightweight annual climbers, such as beans, sugar snap peas and mangetouts (snow peas), hybrid berries and sweet peas. They can also be used for the more sprawling types of climber that can take up too much room horizontally, such as squash, baby pumpkins and climbing courgettes (zucchini), but not for training fruits and other permanent shrubs that need a long-term foundation. The panels are normally fixed directly to a wall or fence. Use small pieces of wood as spacers to provide an air gap for the plants to twine.

Screens have a decorative role as well as a functional one, by dividing up the beds and providing a backdrop to other planting. Trellis panels can be employed as free-standing screens for climbing vegetables (see page 63 for the method). Used in this way, light and air can reach all round the plants. Trellis divides can be made using roofing laths and rustic poles, so that the mesh can be made the size you like. Adaptable modular fencing screens are available in different styles – constructed with metal poles and combined with black climbing mesh they give an excellent foundation for climbers.

Right: *A brick path, bordered with leeks, beetroots and marigolds, passes beneath a wooden pergola and trellis divisions entwined with runner bean plants.*

Wattle Hurdles

An alternative to trellis is the more rustic look of wattle hurdles, which suit the productive garden well. There has been a strong revival in country crafts over the past few years, and it is easy these days to source country-style wattle hurdles in a variety of sizes and styles.

The hurdles are rigid panels woven from willow, hazel or chestnut. These make attractive screens and dividers, as well as lending a sense of history. However, quality, and therefore durability, varies enormously, so if you want a product to last for a few years, you should not necessarily opt for the cheapest available.

Hurdles are not primarily used as climbing plant supports, but they are very efficient when employed as boundaries and windbreaks around a vegetable plot. The fine gaps in

the weaving allow air to be filtered through gently, thus avoiding the turbulence that can cause planting problems when solid barriers are used. It also cuts out wind chill and traps sunlight to create a more protected climate for your plants.

Above left: *A woven willow panel provides wind protection, creating a sheltered micro-climate for the young apple tree.*

Above right: *Rustic wattle hurdles make up a low screen fence to separate the potager from the rest of the garden.*

FIXING WATTLE HURDLES

Traditional hurdles can be made from split hazel, chestnut or woven willow wands (the latter are illustrated here). They form a natural-looking backdrop or screen where conventional fencing panels might appear visually jarring. As well as forming a delightful rustic backdrop for fruits and vegetables, you could also use them to screen off a composting area or to set off a border of cottage flowers and herbs. Fix the hurdles to stout wooden posts or, for a modern touch, use aluminium posts.

1 Measure the width of the hurdles and then set fence posts securely into the ground the right distance apart using a quick-drying concrete mix or spiked metal sockets. Then fix one end of the panel to the post by overlapping it and drilling through the hurdle into the post.

2 Use long galvanized screws to attach the hurdles to the posts using the predrilled holes. You can also erect lower hurdles using metal angle irons driven into the ground. Attach the hurdles to the angle irons by threading electrical cable ties through the holes in the metal.

3 Attach the other end of the panel to the support and continue in the same way to create the fence. Raise the hurdles off the ground to slow down rotting at the base. Hurdles can also be used as temporary garden dividers or boundaries while hedges are still growing.

PLANTS AND CONTAINERS FOR THE EDIBLE GARDEN

Your planting choices need to fit within the fixed perameters of your patio, as well as its aspect and light quality, if your fruit, vegetables and herbs are to flourish. An orderly planting style helps you to identify what is growing where, but a little unruliness with some mixed planting will soften the look.

Above: *These potted succulents create an attractive display outside the kitchen.*

Above: *Raised beds provide extra soil depth for greedy vegetables. These willow planters are filled with tomatoes, artichokes and herbs.*

Choosing Containers

Wooden barrels are ideal planters for vegetables that demand depth of soil. Potatoes, carrots, runner (green) beans and leeks can be grown in deep containers such as old rust-resistant galvanized dustbins or washtubs.

Other ideas for cottage-garden style containers are large, lined metal colanders used as hanging containers. Or, make an all-summer salad garden in old butlers' sinks or stone troughs. Use these to sow successions of colourful salad leaves, from tightly crisp green varieties, such as 'Little Gem' ('Bibb'), through to curvaceous cut-and-come-again picking leaf forms, including 'Salad Bowl', purple 'Lollo Rosso' and red-tinged 'Sangria'.

Edible scented flowers and leaves add spice to salads and rice dishes and are ideal container plants. They give colour and interest to containers with less-attractive fare, such as aromatic herbs or vegetables. Choose mauve and yellow violas, orange and red nasturtiums, or peppery pinks.

Herb Options

If space is limited, use fresh herbs as edgings to border other plants, or sow them in pots. Choose herbs that you like to cook with and that make good garnishes, and those that are expensive to buy or hard to get hold of, such as basil or coriander. Fill a big container with vitamin-packed parsley and another with chives, both of which can be used in large quantities in the kitchen. Choose thyme varieties for their pungent flavours, as well as purple and green sage, upright and creeping rosemary, and marjoram. Mint is rampant in open ground but is also happy to grow in containers.

MAKING A HANGING BASKET

A hanging basket, planted up with a combination of herbs, vegetables, fruits and edible flowers, is ideal where you have limited room for beds or floor-standing containers. Most herbs – including thyme, sage, basil, mint, oregano, parsley and chives – will grow happily in a basket. Other edibles include salad leaves, tumbler tomatoes, and cut-and-come-again vegetables, such as rainbow chard and baby spinach. Hanging baskets are, however, prone to drying out, so you need to water them regularly, at least daily.

1 Before planting, puncture the plastic liner up the sides. Add slow-release fertilizer to good-quality compost (soil mix) and fill two-thirds full.

2 Plant taller elements, such as the rainbow chard, in the centre and then add nasturtiums (*Tropaeolum majus*) to trail over the sides.

3 Plant alpine strawberries, or *fraises des bois*, so they cascade down the sides. Tumbler tomatoes or dwarf French beans are other options.

4 Fill with smaller plants, such as French marigolds. Top up the compost, water and stand in a shady, sheltered spot. Hang on a sheltered wall.

KEEPING A HANGING BASKET

• *If growing tomatoes, give the basket some some midday shade.*
• *Water regularly, deadhead and remove fading leaves to keep plants healthy and productive.*
• *Harvest a little at a time to give plants a chance to regrow.*
• *Feed with liquid tomato fertilizer from mid-summer.*
• *Keep small pots of replacement salads, annual herbs and edible flowers available. Remove the dead plants and add the new ones.*
• *Cut off the flowering stems of leaf vegetables and herbs grown for foliage, such as parsley and mint.*
• *In winter: take down the basket; cut perennial plants back to tidy them; pinch off dead leaves; and remove annuals. Stand the basket in the top of a large plant pot at the base of a sheltered wall. Replant, refresh the potting mix and add new varieties in the spring.*

Left: *You are unlikely to forget to water a hanging basket that is located just outside the kitchen door.*

PLANTING A STRAWBERRY URN

Strawberries are enjoyed for the colour they bring to the garden, as well as their sweet taste. The strawberry urn has small side pockets or openings that hold the small plants, and allow the plants to bear fruit using the full depth of the container. The container must have drainage holes in the bottom of the pot, critical in order to keep the roots from rotting. When the planting is finished, be sure to position the urn in full sun.

1 You will need to wet an urn made from terracotta, because otherwise the clay will wick the water out of the soil. Either place the urn in a tub of water for about an hour, or hose and wet the urn. You can get strawberry urns in plastic, but the terracotta ones are more attractive.

2 Put about 2.5cm (1in) of your soil in the bottom of the container and then cover this lightly with a layer of pea gravel or small rocks or broken crockery. This will help with drainage.

3 Continue to fill the urn with soil until you reach the lowest level of pockets. Insert one of the strawberry plants in each of the lower pockets, filling around them with soil and firming it gently. Make sure the crown of the plants is just above the soil level.

4 Water the lower level and each newly planted pocket. Fill the urn with soil until you reach the next level of pockets. Repeat the planting process. As you do this, place a 2.5cm (1in) PVC pipe drilled with holes down the centre of the pot so that each plant gets adequate moisture.

5 Stop adding soil when you get to 5cm (2in) below the rim of the pot. You can then add three to four plants in the very top of the container, and fill in with soil around them.

6 During the growing season, water the plant at each side opening, as well as the plants in the top layer. Keep the soil moist but not soggy. Every two weeks, apply a half-monthly amount of complete fertilizer. Special strawberry pots such as the one pictured are made with planting pockets.

Plants for your Productive Garden

To ensure an extended growing season, plant a good variety of perennial and annual flowers alongside your edible produce, such as cheerful winter pansies that will go on flowering through the low months. An abundance of climbers will also give vertical interest. Fill containers with brightly coloured flowers.

Insects and birds will flock to the pollen-laden blooms of mallows, rosemary, lavender and honeysuckle, and to the energy-giving seedheads of poppies and love-in-a-mist, helping propagation and pest control.

Companion Planting

Certain combinations of herbs and vegetables benefit from each other by encouraging healthy growth and diverting attention from unwanted pests. For example, tomatoes like to be planted alongside lemon balm and borage, which in turn encourages bees to aid in pollination. Parsley is good to tomatoes, carrots, asparagus and chives. Basil is the perfect table

companion to tomatoes, and a few pots around the doorway will discourage flies and mosquitoes. Plant garlic near your fruit trees to repel pests.

Above: *Teeming with produce, this corner bed includes curly kale,* Hemerocallis *'Stella de Oro', strawberry, globe artichoke, French marigolds, Lollo Rosso lettuce, fennel, red cabbage, corn and borage.*

MAKING A STONE TROUGH

Solid stone troughs, such as old butlers' sinks, are difficult to source at a reasonable price, as well as being heavy to move about. Simulated ones, however, can be made with an artificial stone mixture or hypertufa.

Here, a glazed sink is coated to give it an authentic cottage-garden appeal. Once completed, the 'stone' trough could be used for planting herbs and salads, as well as other plant varieties.

1 Stand the sink on a narrower plinth so the coating does not stick to the support. If using a glazed sink, score the glazed surface with a tile-cutter to give the coating grip.

2 Coat the sink with industrial glue and leave it until it has gone tacky. Mix equal parts of sphagnum peat or peat substitute, sand or grit and cement, adding water slowly.

3 Wearing rubber gloves, apply the mixture, or hypertufa, working from the bottom up. The covering should be just thick enough to give a rough texture.

4 Cover the sink with plastic sheeting for up to a week until it is dry. Paint the hypertufa with liquid fertilizer to encourage the growth of mosses and make it look older.

STRUCTURES FOR THE EDIBLE GARDEN

Exploit the vertical dimension of your patio to utilize every available space. Boundaries offer instant backdrops for fruit trees and climbers, while arbours and arches, and temporary features such as willow wigwams, offer a multitude of edible and decorative possibilities, as well as offering extra privacy.

Above: *A hazel wigwam makes a support for abundantly fruiting cherry tomatoes.*

Left: *Apple trees trained over a pergola, protecting a patio seating area.*

Above: *A steel arch framework makes a good support for vines and climbing squashes, or for training pears.*

Structures for Training Produce

Edible produce trained over a timber arbour, or pergola, fixed along a house or boundary wall, creates a cloistered dining area with a special appeal. Trained with a grapevine, a pergola will provide shade in summer and cascades of luscious fruit for the table in autumn.

For a patio garden in a warmer climate, the Chinese gooseberry, *Actinidia chinensis*, twines vigorous, hairy stems to support show-off handsome, architectural foliage and a crop of juicy kiwi fruits.

A wrought-iron or timber gazebo is another good permanent structure for training fruit or vegetables. Make the gazebo from rustic poles topped with a hazel branch roof to shelter a twisted timber seat. Plant it up with unconventional soft fruits, such as thornless blackberry or tayberry, for a late summer crop for pies and jellies, or an ornamental vine with autumn colour, such as *Vitis* 'Brandt'.

Arches and Tunnels

A simple double arch made from steel or timber provides a framework for training a variety of climbing plants. This could make an excellent entrance point for a pathway or a dramatic framing device.

You could introduce a succession of arches linked with wires, to create a tunnel walk. Planting possibilities would then include yellow climbing squash, ornamental gourds or baby orange pumpkin, runner (green) beans, climbing nasturtiums or sweetpeas for cutting. Purple climbing French beans look and taste good, while the glamorous hyacinth bean, *Lablab purpureus*, is a true prima donna; its cerise flowers are followed by enormously long, gleaming, purple pods that are edible, and also make superb decoration. These, together with squash and small fruited pumpkin, require a very warm and sunny situation.

BUILDING A SIMPLE PERGOLA

You can buy pergola kits at larger home-improvement stores, garden centres and nurseries. The kits include all the fixings and brackets you need, as well as the timber pieces pre-cut for easy assembly. It is also possible to buy the various elements separately for modular constructions. In the sequence here, uncut timbers and fence posts have been used to make a cube-shaped pergola. This small structure would make an ideal spot for enjoying the fruits of your labours and by fixing trellis panels and overhead wires you could clothe the pergola with climbing fruits and vines. Thornless blackberries, for example, cover a large area in no time and combine pretty flowers with a succession of fruits. Try growing grapes or kiwi fruit overhead.

1 Excavate a 45–60cm (18–24in) deep hole using a trenching spade and post-hole tongues. Water the base, add dry, ready-mixed post-hole concrete. Ram the concrete to consolidate it and water in.

2 Start with 2.5–3m (9–10ft), 10cm (4in) uprights, so that the finished pergola allows head room of 2.3m (7ft 6in). Use a crosspiece and a spirit (carpenter's) level to check the post is perfectly level.

3 Check the right angles using a builder's set square and lay the long joists on the ground to calculate the distance and position required for the next post-hole to be dug.

4 Using a 5 x 10cm (2 x 4in) crosspiece with a spirit level between two adjacent posts, check that each of the four uprights are perpendicular and level. Rectify any errors now.

5 Lay the first crosspiece over two pillars and, allowing for a generous overhang, mark on the timber the width and position of the upright fence post to locate the notched fixing.

6 Secure the beam on a workbench and, using a saw, cut down into the notch to create four segments. Then use a sharp wood chisel to remove each segment, as shown here.

7 Lock the crosspiece in place at both ends and pre-drill holes through to the uprights. Fix the crossbeam with 70mm (2¾in) galvanized screws. Repeat this process for the parallel crossbeam.

8 Taking two more identical pieces of wood, measure the positions of the crossing beams and saw and chisel out notches as before. Fix this second set of beams securely in place.

9 Edge the base of the pergola with timber, securing it to the posts and, after removing the turf and laying a landscape membrane, surface the floor area with bark chippings or gravel.

Forged steel is the most suitable and enduring material from which to make a curved profile shape for such structures, although cheaper plastic-tube systems that can be adapted to many heights and lengths are also available.

It is possible to have a bespoke curved timber arch made to your specifications. Such an addition to the garden would certainly be very beautiful, but the cost would also be high. Wood is more usually found in square profile, using upright posts for support with a slatted roof. In a kitchen garden, the rustic pole concept is practical, cheap and very much in keeping with a country style. This would make a perfect foil for climbing runner (green) beans; to make a real impact, try pink-flowered 'Sunset', white 'Desiree' and 'Painted Lady' splashed with both red and white.

On a smaller scale, there are support staging structures on the market that provide effective growing frames. In combination with a standard growbag, such vertical frames will support heavier fruits and vegetables that like to grow vertically.

Above: *A staged support structure for tomatoes makes the most of a small space.*

Raised Beds

You can experience two main difficulties when creating a vegetable plot in an enclosed space: poor soil and insufficient light. Creating raised beds within retaining walls should, however, help to remedy both problems at once – first, by increasing soil depth and, second, by bringing the plants out into the light.

Retaining walls made of brick are good-looking, though fairly costly. Reduce the expense by using

Above: *A small wooden potting bench, with raised edges to retain loose soil.*

Left: *Raised beds provide additional soil depth and bring plants nearer to the light.*

concrete blocks, but you will then need to give them a decorative finish of some type to improve their distinctly utilitarian appearance.

Finishes include render and paint, or you could face them with terracotta tiles or clad them with woven wattle, depending on the style of their surroundings. However, for a simpler and more straightforward form of construction, you could make the walls of the raised beds from reclaimed railway sleepers (ties) or some other heavy timbers (see below).

Good soil drainage is vital for raised beds, so you will need to build on open ground that has been cleared of perennial weeds and dig it over to break up the soil. Don't forget to create drainage holes with pipes near the base of the walls to take away surplus water.

Raised beds must be filled with good-quality topsoil incorporating generous quantities of bulky organic matter, such as garden compost (soil mix), manure or composted bark. The success of your crops depends on this foundation.

Above: *Heavy, sawn timber planks make it easy to construct good-looking raised beds.*

MAKING A RAISED BED WITH SLEEPERS

In a small garden space you have to ensure that even the practical areas are attractive. Meeting both these requirements is this type of raised bed, ideal for growing vegetables and herbs. Railway sleepers (ties) are used to create a low retaining wall. Their weight and stability make construction easy, and only minimal foundations are required. Modern sleepers are usually tanalized, so line the inside with plastic to prevent soil contamination.

1 A chain saw or circular saw is the only practical way to cut sleepers. If you don't feel confident using a saw like this, ask the supplier to cut the sleepers to size for you.

2 To avoid wastage, make a bed that requires least cutting. Lay out the first course of sleepers in a recessed trench filled with hardcore and then start building up.

3 As you build up the layers, arrange the timbers so that the corner joins on adjacent layers don't correspond. Overlapping the timber like this gives extra stability.

4 Use corner brackets as shown in the four corners of at least the top layer of sleepers. This layer is the one most likely to be sat on, leant over and knocked.

5 Fill the bed with sieved (strained), weed-free topsoil mixed with well-rotted manure or compost (soil mix). If using tanalized timber, line the sides with heavy-duty plastic to avoid contamination.

RAISED BED CROSS-SECTION

railway sleepers

topsoil and organic manure mix

ground level compacted hardcore

WORKADAY ORNAMENT FOR THE EDIBLE GARDEN

Using 'ornamental' features in a productive space is not the contradiction you may think. Utilitarian features often have a character that fits with their purpose – displayed antique tools, attractively age-worn implements and containers, and structures for feeding or sheltering animals.

Above: *Even a tiny residence like this can house a surprising number of white doves.*

Above: *An old basket, here used for tending aromatic basil and tomato plants, creates an attractive picture.*

Utilitarian Features

Everyday gardening hand tools are the ornament of a productive garden. Spades, forks, rakes and hoes have a functional beauty in their own right, whether brightly shining stainless steel, exclusive horn-handled varieties or simply those you have collected over the years. Choose your tools carefully, checking their weight, balance and quality, and look after them, cleaning and oiling regularly.

Old garden and farmyard implements can be found in junk shops and fairs. Weathered zinc watering cans, buckets and milk churns are decorative and evocative. Return these tools to daily practical use. If they are too battered, turn leaky holes to advantage by transforming them into planting containers. A discarded domestic

Above: *Characterful tools such as these give enormous pleasure in their daily use.*

water tank makes an excellent rainwater butt; you might combine it with a cascading fountain feature, using old watering cans.

Pieces of rusted farm machinery can be given a new lease of life, used as a three-dimensional plant support for climbing beans, or as a stand-alone sculpture by a planting bed. Antique, long handled rakes, spades and forks can be fashioned into a distinctive, cross-bar garden gate or fixed on a wall to train annual climbers. Rusty chains, dangled from a wall or canopy, make excellent supports for scramblers and tendril climbers such as sweetpeas. The possibilities for reinventing discarded objects are limitless.

Above: *A redundant galvanized tank transforms to garden butt and fountain feature, conserving precious rainwater.*

Above: *Recycled tins sprayed in bright colours make ornamental herb planters.*

Above: *Old metal pots and buckets make useful planters.*

Above: *Provide a number of seed and nut feeders to attract a wide variety of birds.*

Welcoming Wild Creatures

Visiting wild creatures are a natural part of the potager. The garden life cycle needs earthworms, butterflies, greenfly and slugs to feed birds, aerate the ground and pollinate flowers. So choose plants that attract insects, and avoid pesticides and herbicides that could harm your garden visitors. Birds can be easily attracted with a range of treats including seed mixes, nuts, fat balls, suet cakes and fresh fruit. Maintain a regular feeding routine with tables, seed dispensers and nesting boxes in a quiet place where they are easy to see, which will encourage birds to return to your patio.

HOW TO AGE CONTAINERS

• *To age a terracotta pot, soak it and stand in a damp, shady place to build up a coating of green algae.*
• *To rust a galvanized bucket, follow the steps below, using rust-coloured acrylic paint in place of aqua-green.*

CREATING VERDIGRIS, RUST AND LEAD EFFECTS

The luminous, blue-green tones of weathered copper (verdigris) are simple to reproduce on metal and matt plastic containers. Here we have used a cheap, galvanized bucket. But any recycled metal container such as an old flower arranger's bucket, a recycled olive oil can or a large colander (where you will need to fit chains and line it with plastic), could be transformed, making a decorative rustic container for salads, herbs or strawberries.

1 Sand the surface of the bucket and then prime (paint) it with a metal primer. Allow to dry thoroughly for about two to three hours. Next, apply gold paint and allow that to dry as well for another two to three hours.

2 Paint with amber-coloured shellac and allow it to dry. Mix up some white artist's acrylic paint in aqua-green and add water to make a watery consistency. This will give the colour known as verdigris.

3 Sponge some of the aqua verdigris paint on and allow it to dry for one or two hours. Use a kitchen towel or rag to dab off excess before it is dry. Seal and protect the finish with a coat of matt polyurethane varnish.

4 To use the bucket as a planter, turn it upside down and make drainage holes with a 15cm (6in) nail. Part-fill with gravel before adding compost (soil mix). Plant a row of buckets with purple cabbage, lavender or chives.

WATER FOR THE EDIBLE GARDEN

Water is essential in the kitchen garden to irrigate your crops. You will need to decide on an effective and reliable watering system that suits you and sustains your plants. Watering by hand is convenient, but not always the best option. You can also save rainwater by storing it in a rainwater butt and recycle greywater from the house so that this resource is not wasted.

Above: *A seep hose has minute holes along one side of a plastic or rubber pipe.*

Watering Fruit and Vegetables

Productive crops are especially thirsty and irregular watering will reduce the crops of most vegetables – so you will need an effective and regular watering system. The beginning and the end of the day are the best times to water. Water your crops deeply, and allow the soil time to dry a little before watering again. Light watering can do more harm than no water at all. This is because it stimulates the plant roots to come to the surface, where they are damaged by sun exposure.

Overhead watering is effective if you work within these guidelines. However, the wet foliage that this creates can encourage diseases to settle. A controlled watering system reduces water wastage and supplies water to the base of the plants, just where they need it. A leaky-pipe, seep or soaker hose, is made of recycled rubber and is easy to install in a raised bed (see opposite) and allows water to slowly permeate the soil.

Another effective way to water a vegetable garden is to use a drip or trickle irrigation system, available as kits, connected to an automatic timer. This works well for vegetables that are spaced far apart and for container gardens sited on a deck or terrace. Small tubes are inserted into holes in the main hose line at intervals and water is distributed at low pressure wherever the tubes are placed.

Water Storage

Use a rainwater butt to collect roof water via a drainpipe. Plants prefer rainwater, so you will be doing your fruit trees and vegetables a real favour. The simplest above-ground container is a plastic tank with a spout and tap near the base. These are functional, but not terribly attractive to look at; you may prefer a resin replica of a tall oil jar or stone column if that suits the style of your garden space. Site the container in a shady spot to help preserve the quality of the water inside.

An industrial zinc water tank, even though it is completely utilitarian in appearance, could be made to look less jarring and appear to better integrate into its surroundings if it is partially obscured with plantings of ferns and other shade-loving specimens.

Wooden barrels that have been sealed to retain water can be used in a similar way. A complete barrel would be large enough to function as an irrigation tank in its own right, while a lower, half-barrel could be used to house a fountain feature.

Above: *When using a watering can, water your crops deeply and regularly.*

Above: *Large beer and wine casks make excellent water-storage butts.*

Above: *This water butt has a tap for easy access to the recycled water.*

IRRIGATING A RAISED BED

Watering vegetables, or other bed plants, overhead with a hose could make them more susceptible to disease, because foliage that stays moist too long can cause fungus. A practical and easy way to irrigate raised beds is to combine a soaker hose and a regular hose using a hose connector. This system will ensure that your raised bed plants get a good deep soaking where they need it, and that the foliage stays dry.

1 Mark on your wooden garden frame where the entry point of the irrigation hose should be. In one end of the raised bed, drill a hole that is just large enough to accommodate a standard size hose.

2 Calculate the lengths of garden hose required to cover the distance from each raised bed to the connector (see next step) and from the connector to the water source. Having purchased the hose, cut into shorter lengths to suit these calculations.

3 Use a two-way hose connector valve with built-in shut-offs. These valves connect one or more hoses to the spigot, or to each other. Having a shut-off valve in each connector arm means you can redirect the water flow. Using female hose couplings, attach two pieces of hose.

4 Insert the other ends of the short pieces of hose through the holes you drilled. Inside the raised bed, attach the short pieces of hose to whatever length of soaker hose you need. Outside the bed, attach another length of hose using a female hose coupling.

5 Arrange the soaker hoses in the raised bed in an S-shape to distribute the water. Arrange them at the base of the plants in the row so that water is distributed evenly over the plant roots. If you prefer not to see the soaker hoses, it is fine to bury them beneath the soil.

IRRIGATION TECHNIQUES

- *Use watering systems such as canvas soaker hoses, perforated plastic sprinkle hoses and drip-type irrigation that ensure water gets where it is most needed. These systems disperse water in a long, narrow pattern that is ideal for beds. Drip irrigation has the advantage of wasting less water.*
- *Water your beds regularly and frequently – effective drainage in a raised bed means that overwatering is minimized, but problems linked to underwatering are increased, especially in deep beds.*
- *Bear in mind that the amount and frequency of watering depends on the water-holding capacity of the soil, weather conditions and the preferences of your plants.*

A PEACEFUL OASIS

The pace of modern life leaves us with a need to find peace and tranquillity. This can be achieved in a patio or terrace with an inspiring and sympathetic planting, natural textures and the relaxed design of the contemplative retreat.

Some elements from this style are borrowed from the restrained aesthetics of oriental garden design, characterized by a pared-down, natural approach. An effective patio haven will provide spiritual nourishment as well as physical relaxation, giving you the space and surroundings in which to pause, be still and reflect. It will bring you close to nature, helping you to understand and appreciate the rhythm and cycles of the seasons, revcaling new shoots, flowers, fruits and seeds. Nurturing the soil and its plants forms part of this healing process, providing a way of refreshing your spirit and calming your mind.

Left: *A textured palette of green and grey shrubs and flowers encompasses the seating area and creates a delightful, protected and restorative outdoor refuge.*

FLOORING FOR A PEACEFUL SPACE

Select natural, unprocessed materials for floors in this soothing, simple patio. Untreated timbers and rough-hewn stones are key materials to use as floors. Naturally textured and weathered surfaces help to give the impression that materials evolved from the site, and designing in flowing lines creates a calming atmosphere.

Above: *A coat of varnish brings out the grain of rough-sawn softwood.*

Gravel, Pebbles and Chippings

The loose nature and crunchy texture of gravel provides a low-key surface that suits an organic design. Gravel is a term that covers a range of stone aggregate in varying sizes. Most often it is applied to pea shingle, which is quarried from riverbeds. Shingle is inexpensive, readily available and excellent for paths and large background areas. Stone chippings are tiny pieces of marble, limestone or granite mostly used as a decorative mulch.

Beach pebbles make an elegant alternative for surfacing. Sea-washed smooth, their subtle colours vary in tone through cream, pink and grey to almost black. Sizes are graded from a few millimetres – ideal for paths – to generously proportioned

cobbles – an excellent complement to water features and plantations of grasses. Combine pebbles in different sizes to make an integrated design. To define a path of small-grade stones, line the edges with pebbles of a larger size to add texture and to hold back the planting on either side. Strew mounds of large cobbles to make sculptural 'beds' that contrast with simple screen planting beyond, and throw in an occasional giant stone for extra effect. Make a rocky beach surround for a natural pond, grading the sizes gradually down to the water's edge.

Slate chippings make a handsome alternative. Their form is reminiscent of scree and so produces more of a mountainside effect in contrast to

Above: *A pathway of recycled, green-coloured glass stones, edged with brick, picks up on the surrounding plant greenery.*

that of the beach, while its mossy colours of green and plum make it an excellent complement to naturalistic planting.

Fine, crushed slate makes a subtle decorative mulch, while chunky 40mm (1⅛in) pieces can be used for heavier duty areas, such as walkways. It is perhaps most successful when employed to create a dry river bed effect, mimicking a stream snaking down a slope. Although pebbles can be used instead, slate's darker tone is more reminiscent of water and is effective when wet, the hillside colours taking on an extra intensity.

Above: *Boulders, rocks and beach pebbles achieve a texturally interesting pathway.*

Above: *Smooth, oblong limestone slabs create a cool-looking terrace around this fountain feature.*

Solid Surfaces

Blocks of dark granite would be a classic choice, but other stones of character can be used, too. Thick slabs of slate would look especially handsome when wet, while an Indian sandstone containing fossil remains would demonstrate its primeval origins. Heavy rocks may also be used to suggest an imaginary path through foliage that is not intended for a physical passage.

Stone offers obvious natural connections with the earth, but wood is also an interesting material in the contemplative garden. Trees grow from the earth so timber will reconnect us by providing walkways. Blocks of heavy wood, used like stepping-stones, will have a powerful visual impact, introducing textural contrast to gravel paths.

Where slopes and changes of level are encountered, thick wooden planks can be used to retain the soil on the bank, and the surfaces covered with gravel to create shallow steps.

Gravel has a tendency to shift when walked on, so the timber will also serve to secure the aggregate to make walking easier. Sawn-up railway sleepers (ties) or reclaimed structural beams are ideal for the purpose, while large pieces of driftwood would add a sculptural quality. Sink them into the ground so they sit at just the finished height of the surrounding aggregate.

Above: *Weathered timber planks create a secure, textural transition across pebbles.*

upward dimension. The concept works well if it creates a passage across or alongside a pond or stretch of water, providing a haven for wildlife. Where it is not feasible to build a pond, the impression of bog garden can be just as visually effective. Plant an area with tall reeds and grasses, which will produce evocative rustling sounds and drooping seedheads and push the walkway through them.

In place of the boardwalk, you might prefer to install a timber viewing deck. This would be an ideal device on a hillside plot to take advantage of any vistas below. If you are thinking of making a pool, a deck provides a practical seating area, especially if it is cantilevered out over the water, enabling you to feel closer to nature and more part of the wildlife environment. Another idea involving wood is to build a low, raised bed from railroad sleepers (ties) (see also page 97).

Paths and Walkways

The main role of the path in a contemplative garden design is to create a slow, meandering journey, allowing time for reflection. It should not be possible to see the destination immediately, but little vistas should open up along the way. A Japanese-style path made of loose-laid stepping-stones would provide an excellent textural contrast to either a gravel or a grassy track, while also making a sympathetic and practical walkway. Choose bold slabs of stone in similar but irregular sizes with random edges and profiles for the most natural effect.

Boardwalks can introduce a fascinating element to this style of garden. The timber planks are very much in keeping, and by raising the pathway on stilts you create a new

Above: *Rocks and boulders can create the effect of a dried-up stream bed.*

Above: *Loose-laid stepping-stones bedded into grass create a more natural pathway solution than conventional paving in concrete.*

MAKING A PEBBLE BEACH FEATURE

Swirling patterns and textures created with natural materials can make pleasing features for the contemplative garden. This stylized, free-flowing design takes its inspiration from the wave-form ceramic plaque, but also symbolizes the opposing yet complementary forces of yin and yang. You could easily centre the design on a circular stepping-stone with Japanese or Chinese lettering, or on a shallow ceramic serving dish filled with water, which could double as a birdbath. Alternatively, work the pebbles around a tall, rough-hewn rock.

1 Decide precisely where the main elements are to go, including any pot groupings, the centrepiece and the large, water-worn boulders. Bed the centrepiece and boulders down into the gravel slightly to give them more of a natural, established appearance.

2 Pour a bag of cobbles, in muted browns and greys, into the gaps between the boulders. These don't need to be precisely arranged, as they will form the backdrop and unifying element of the feature. Part burying the boulders mimics the look of a natural beach.

3 Continue covering the ground with a sack of grey speckled granite cobbles. A few of these should also be placed on top of the cobbles to blend the transition. Alternatively, use the same muted brown and grey colours, but in a smaller pebble size, and mix as before.

4 Using shingle, fill the gaps between the larger stones and blend in the edges to link them with the original background of gravel. Note that it is illegal to collect gravel or pebbles from a beach without the permission of the landowner.

5 Finally create a dramatic swirling waveform that winds through the feature using sparkling white pebbles. This flourish tails off between the plants and pots. Thin the pebbles at the edges to create the suggestion of sea foam.

6 With split bamboo and brushwood screening at the rear making a uniform backdrop, and using oriental-style plants such as sedges and bamboo, this feature would fit into an oriental scheme or even a narrow side passage or balcony space.

WALLS AND SCREENS FOR A PEACEFUL SPACE

A sense of enclosure is an important aspect of a peaceful oasis. Walls and partitions can use a soft natural material, such as bamboo, or shiny and reflective surfaces can add an air of mystery. Less sympathetic partitions can be broken up with other devices, such as fabric screens and obscuring greenery.

Above: *The raffia panel, intended to mark a pathway, drifts atmospherically in the breeze.*

Above: *A plain wall with a liquid crystal panel is set off by a stand of tall bamboo, making a serene backdrop to this area.*

Bamboo Screening

Traditionally, Japanese screening is made from cut bamboo poles tied together with black string. Such screens can be purchased ready made, but quality ones can be expensive. This is a viable project to do yourself if you can find poles of a suitable diameter, around 3–5cm (1¼–2in). Arrange them in a diagonal diamond pattern and tie them together with identical knots using heavy-duty, tarred garden twine in place of the traditional black string.

Above: *Ready-made bamboo screening is fixed to supports, creating a lightweight screen.*

Bamboo is relatively weather resistant, but keep it away from the ground or it will rot. For this reason, secure the panels to preserved timber posts concreted into the ground. This will give you an open screen to define an area or provide a backdrop.

Where a more solid screen is required you can create a framework of preserved timber slats on which to build your screen. You will need vertical posts set into the ground, with two horizontal rails set at around 15–20cm (6–8in) from the finished dimensions at the top and bottom, on which to fix vertically the bamboo poles. Pre-drill holes through the poles and fix them to the timber rails with brass screws or more economical stainless-steel-headed nails.

Ready-made bamboo screening is available by the roll, so simply fix the screening directly to your basic framework using wire ties or twine. This lighter-weight system is suitable for use as a wind shelter. It is made either from wooden posts (see method opposite) or fine bamboo stems held together with steel wire.

Lightweight raffia panels can make an airy, ephemeral statement. Suspend them from one side, letting them fly freely in the breeze – high up and horizontally to emphasize an area, or vertically to mark a pathway.

A screen wall of living bamboo gives an entirely different effect, combining green foliage with stems ranging from bright yellow and green to black. Bamboo can be invasive so if you are concerned, commercial root-retaining barriers are available by the roll.

Above: *Cut stems of silver birch saplings create a delicate semi-open screen.*

Right: *Bamboo will suffer from wet and rot if pushed directly into the ground; these canes are fixed to a timber framework to create an elegant and durable fence.*

CREATING A BAMBOO FENCE

The design and construction of bamboo fences and screens in Japan is a highly specialized art, but if you prefer a more instant solution then buy ready-made screens, or follow these steps. The materials here are widely available and you can create an authentic look without having to purchase expensive imported goods.

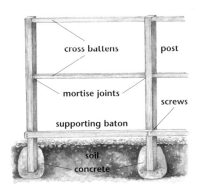

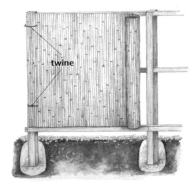

1 Set posts 1.5–2m (5–6½ft) apart. Dig holes up to 45–50cm (18–20in) deep by 20cm (8in) wide. Concrete the posts in place, screwing on the lower baton 4cm (1½in) off the ground. Chisel out mortises in the posts for the cross battens halfway up the posts and at the top of the posts. Screw the joints into the posts.

2 Support the roll of ready-made bamboo fencing material on the lower supporting batten, temporarily attaching one end of it to a post with some twine. Unroll the fencing material, attaching it to the cross battens with twine.

3 Hold the bamboo in place using facing boards screwed on to the posts. Cut the posts level with the bamboo. Lay capping boards over the post tops, both for their appearance and to stop rain getting into the end grain, and screw them down. Stain them ash black to provide a contrast with the bamboo fencing material.

Right: Fine textile panels, held taut by thin battens at the top and bottom, provide shade without totally obscuring the light and the view.

Creating the Mood

Screening does not have to follow a traditional route – contemporary alternatives can give a special look without departing from the natural theme that suits the contemplative style. It is invariably the distressed, the worn and the patinated surface that fits comfortably in a thoughtful, peaceful space, and even quite modern materials take on this quality over time. Metal panels can be used as backdrops or walls and, when oxidizing, can evolve into organic colours and textures. Copper will transform from its burnished hues to give a greenish, verdigris effect. Zinc will change from dark grey to a whitish, powdery finish that works well with subtle foliage, while steel will rust into delicious, orangy tones. Pressed metal panels constructed from aluminium, galvanized iron, copper or zinc can be used outdoors as a feature decoration on a foundation wall.

A glass screen, etched with a suitable design, can produce a visual pause in the garden, while not interrupting the view beyond. Textiles will deliver a similar effect if they are translucent and gauze-like, while dense fabrics will hide and enclose.

Bear in mind that any solid material will stop wind temporarily, while at the same time causing turbulence. Fixings should therefore be securely attached with some sort of spacing between the panels to aid the passage of strong breezes.

Above: *The wavy relief in this translucent glass screen suggests gently flowing rain.*

Above: *These succulents are attached to a wire mesh covered with a water-retentive fibre.*

Above: *Floaty muslin screens drift from this rustic pergola to create an intimate corner.*

IDEAS FOR BOUNDARIES IN A PEACEFUL SPACE

• *Keep the visual effect of enclosures light to avoid overpowering the garden.*
• *Screen walls can be made in sections of solid material, such as rendered blocks or painted marine ply, allowing planting spaces between.*
• *Fix cut bamboo to a timber framework to keep the canes from touching the wet ground; tie the poles in latticework layouts using black string to replicate Japanese designs.*
• *Plant newly pruned stems of willow such as Salix viminalis in winter to create a permanent living screen; weave it into a latticework design for extra density and interest.*
• *Panels of woven 'dead' willow make useful temporary screens.*

Above: *Fretwork trees echo the distant olive, creating interesting silhouettes to highlight the screen wall and planting beds.*

Below: *Solid walls can have figurative elements built in, and this imaginative example fits with a contemplative style.*

PLANTS AND CONTAINERS FOR A PEACEFUL SPACE

Whatever other elements you have decided on, it is the inclusion of plants that will bring your peaceful patio to life. This does not necessarily require a profusion of greenery. An abstract and meditative design can be dramatically created with the sparing and symbolic use of tree and plant forms.

Above: *Spiky* Dasylirion serratifolium *and tropical* Vriesia *make interesting highlights.*

Designing with Neutral Spaces

To achieve a balance between planting and hard landscape, it is important to include areas of visual 'resting' space. In a Western garden, this function is usually fulfilled by areas of lawn, and sometimes with paving, but with an oriental interpretation an area of smooth pebbles can provide a similar calming effect. Movement and texture are achieved by raking them into a curved design to suggest an undulating landscape or ripples in a lake, as in a traditional Zen viewing garden. A variation on this theme might be to use large, carefully chosen containers and specimen plants to create graphic statements, rather than the traditional large-scale boulders that are associated with this garden style.

Balancing Hard and Soft

A purely stone garden can seem cool and impassive to Western eyes, so it is desirable to incorporate some living 'forest' elements for vegetative relief. Retain the original concept by restricting them to focus on sculptural accents, rather than spreading them around too liberally. Static, clipped evergreens and low mounds of green moss provide sculptural form, while clumps of *Festuca* and sedge grasses offer swaying movement.

Choosing Pots

Containers provide an important transition between the garden and the house, so select them in line with the oriental influences of a peaceful patio. There is a good selection of stoneware planters on

the market, sometimes glazed in celadon green, smouldering blue and mysterious plum. Alternatively, deep, burned-brown raku glazes have the right weatherbeaten look for the effect you want to create. Stoneware is usually frost-proof, but do check.

Pots are sometimes made without drainage holes, making them suitable for water-loving species, such as papyrus grass or Marsh marigolds (*Caltha palustris*). A water-filled stoneware bowl will provide a miniature 'pond' if there is no space for the real thing and a lovely vessel for floating beautiful cut blooms. Don't leave water in containers in winter if it is likely to freeze. Tall, oriental water jars look handsome in their own right – not needing a plant for adornment – and make an excellent sculptural statement set among foliage.

Sculptured Forms

Trimming and pruning play an important part in creating sculptural forms. While in the West we commonly use topiary shrub forms, such as box and yew, the Japanese prune conifers into symbolic shapes, often referred to as 'cloud pruning'.

Evergreen pine trees are revered as symbols of stability and endurance. The Japanese black pine, *Pinus thunbergii*, and red pine, *P. densiflora*, are both available in dwarf cultivars and will stand up to the necessary training and pruning. Prostrate and pendulous forms of pines, such as *P. strobus* 'Nana' and

Above: *Low-growing clumping grasses give a soft interface between two paving areas.*

Above: *The streaky patina of the zinc planter combines well with the grey lavender.*

P. densiflora 'Pendula', are ideal for sculpted courtyards, particularly in conjunction with gravel and rock areas. Sculptural subjects can also be found among other conifers, with the spruces, *Picea* sp., offering attractive dwarf forms.

Dramatic sculptural form can also be provided by the New Zealand tree fern, *Dicksonia antarctica*, with its bold, fibrous trunk and broad canopy of fresh green fronds. Although they are considered tender, these ferns frequently flourish in the shelter of a patio. If suitable climatic conditions for *Dicksonia antarctica* do not prevail, the Chinese fan palm (*Trachycarpus fortunei*), and the Mediterranean fan palm (*Chamerops humilis*), offer a similar visual effect.

Right: *Sculptural planting, such as these clipped azaleas in a sea of gravel, brings poise and drama to the scene.*

PLANTING A GRAPE HYACINTH

Create a dreamy blue cascade by planting several varieties of honey-scented grape hyacinth (ones flowering at the same time) in each pot and lining the garden steps with them. Or, cluster the pots together to make a textural blue carpet to brighten the earliest weeks of the year. When the flowers are spent, don't discard the bulbs – take them out of their pots and plant them in clumps in the garden where they will flower happily next spring.

1 Line the base of a shallow pot with a layer of stone chippings to allow free drainage. Taller pots will need a deeper layer of drainage material. You can grow the bulbs in a sheltered corner of the garden before moving them on show. They are hardy and easy to grow.

2 Half-fill the pot with soil-based potting mix and place the bulbs, equally spaced, across the surface. Use seven bulbs for a 12cm (4¾in) pot; nine for a 15cm (6in) pot. Discard any bulbs that are shrivelled or soft. It is easier to make a pleasant arrangement using odd numbers of bulbs.

3 Fill to 2cm (¾in) from the top of the pot with more soil mix and firm lightly. Water the pots using a watering can with a fine rose. From planting time in early autumn, through winter, check watering needs. Top up with a layer of gravel or slate to acts as a foil for the bulbs when they flower.

4 A display like this will continue for several weeks if watered regularly and will attract the first butterflies and bees with their rich nectar. Once the flowers begin to fade, feed the bulbs with a high potash fertilizer, such as tomato food, to build them up for next year.

Contemplative Planting

A patio needs a strong base of evergreens to provide structure throughout the year, but a selection of deciduous species will reflect the changing seasons. The deciduous trees that most epitomize the oriental spirit are the flowering cherries and plums (*Prunus*), which sometimes offer beautiful bark as well as frothy spring blossom. In fact, nothing represents the transition to spring as aptly as cherry blossom. Just one small tree, such as pure-white 'Shirotae', deep-pink 'Cheals Weeping' or scented, shell-pink 'Takasago', is enough to lift the spirits after a long winter.

Space should be found for at least one elegant camellia, offering glossy, evergreen form with glorious blooms in spring. Rich double forms vie with extravagant singles boasting huge bosses of yellow stamens against petals of pure

Above: *Bamboo foliage diffuses light and makes a lovely rattling sound in the breeze.*

Above: *Deep red damask roses amongst a swathe of perennials herald the summer.*

white, rosy pink and deep red. Dwarf rhododendrons and azaleas are important, too, for their kaleidoscope of late spring flowers.

Autumn is the other transitional period, when flowers fade, fruits ripen and leaves prepare to drop. At this time, the brilliant maples (*Acer*) come into their own. Invaluable are the myriad varieties of *A. palmatum*, its deeply lobed foliage turning from bright, springtime green to vibrant tones of yellow, gold and red.

Plants that shiver in the breeze, creating dappled sunlight and evoking the natural landscape, fit perfectly into the contemplative concept. Statuesque bamboos, with their dense clumps of slender stems and wind-clattering leaves, make handsome screens or boundaries.

Ornamental grasses offer a similar effect of swaying stems and rustling leaves. Lower in height than most bamboo, they play an important role, both for edging paths and for making group statements. *Miscanthus sinensis* is a species that offers some of the most beautiful specimens, with fine, arching foliage and gleaming, feathery flower heads in late summer and autumn. Stripy leaved *M. s.* 'Zebrinus', slender 'Gracillimus' and arching 'Kleine Fontäine' are just a few examples.

Left: *Majestic tree ferns* Dicksonia antarctica *create an intimate enclosure with dramatic canopies of foliage.*

Above: *Japanese water iris (*Iris ensata*) is a good foil to the regal fern (*Osmunda regalis*).*

Above: *Large containers that can support a number of plants are ideal for terraces.*

Above: *A small cloud-pruned tree using Japanese holly (*Ilex crenata*).*

To show off their form and the delicacy of the flowers, place them where the low, setting sun provides backlight. For an airy effect, *Molinia arundinacea* and *Stipa tenuissima* both offer feathery pink flowers on arching stems. For contrast, the *Festuca glauca* cultivars offer low, tufted clumps of fine, blue-grey leaves, superb when planted in groups in a sunny spot.

For a still pool of water, low-growing hostas offer a magnificent range of colours enhanced by their deeply veined, glaucous leaves. Blue greens are shot through with acid yellow, spring green is brightened with splashes of cream and white.

Ferns offer sculptural elegance as fronds unfurl to reveal deeply dissected soft, green leaves that deepen in tone as they develop. For

the curiosity of its noduled stems, the horsetail *Equisetum hymale* is hard to beat, with *Juncus effusus spiralis*, the aptly named corkscrew grass, a close second. Among this boggy planting, add white-flowering calla lilies, *Zantedeschia aethiopica*, for their statuesque flower spathes, and Japanese water iris, *Iris laevigata* 'Snowdrift'. Above all, water lilies are transcendentally serene.

HOW TO PRUNE CLOUD TOPIARY

Choose a small-leaved evergreen shrub, such as box (*Buxus sempervirens*), Japanese holly (*Ilex crenata*) or privet (*Ligustrum delavayanum*). You may have a plant with the right 'bone structure', or framework of branches, already growing that would make a suitable candidate. See top right for a trimmed cloud-pruned box.

1 Open up the foliage with both hands to reveal the framework of branches. Ideally, you will have one or more main stems with strong side branches. A quirky branching pattern is ideal.

2 Cut out any unwanted branches, leaving behind more than you will actually need at this stage. Move around the plant and stand back regularly to see how the shape is evolving.

3 Strip the leaves and smaller branches off the lower parts of the main stems you intend to retain for the final shape. Use bamboo canes and wire to bend some branches to the desired shape.

4 Trim the selected stems and side branches at the stem tips to encourage compact growth. Leave bare stem between each 'cloud'. Clip once or twice in spring and summer to maintain its shape.

STRUCTURES AND FURNITURE FOR A PEACEFUL SPACE

A garden is more than flat plane – tall plants and trees, changes of levels, boundaries and enclosures all play their part. To enjoy it fully, the space should evolve into a three-dimensional experience. A reflective space does not require clear divisions, but structural enclosures can create areas of solitude and privacy.

Above: *An archway of hornbeam focuses the view to the topiary forms beyond.*

Arches and Frames

Paths are a good starting point from which to view the garden, especially when they are framed by an archway or other entrance. When designing a garden with a suggestion of the Orient, curved forms provide an evocative vertical device. Frames tend to draw the gaze and can be employed to seduce the viewer to walk towards a destination. More unusual than building a regular, Western-style U-shaped frame, a classical Japanese-style arch would introduce an air of exoticism. The classical form used in temple gardens is based on bold, vertical posts, often round in section, surmounted by one or more carved, horizontal rails. They are sited to permit a symbolic passage from one world to the next. This style of arch is architecturally impressive when used singly, but when interpreted as a series it creates a pergola or covered walkway. This arch can also be adapted to form an enclosure around a bench or seat.

Circles, with their connotations of the Sun and Moon, are frequently used in oriental imagery, and a circular frame would make an effective device to bisect or terminate a pathway. A free-standing circle is quite a challenging object to create, so choose construction materials with care.

Blocks of sandstone or limestone could be used to make a circular frame to be set on a vertical axis. This would be a most impressive feature, although certainly not a construction job for a beginner. To provide a structural support mechanism, the circle would need to be integrated with a screen wall of the same material.

Steel provides the alternative method of construction. Strong and malleable, T- or H-sections can be welded into powerful circular shapes, even large enough to walk through. As with stone

Left: *This cast-iron structure wth a motif of vine leaves has a dream-like quality.*

Right: *Polished stainless steel is becoming a popular medium in the garden. This 'flying' arch creates a dynamic feature, reinforcing the circular patio and swirling mosaic design.*

construction, this should be a job for skilled experts. A single element would be very effective in its own right, but the nature of circles encourages you to site them in different ways. They can be set vertically or at an angle, singly as a frame or as series to suggest a path. They are fascinating formed in groups, especially when organized to achieve a three-dimensional, sculptural effect.

Flat sheet steel could also be used to achieve a different effect. By cutting circular openings in rectangular sections of metal, you can create layers of successive pierced screens.

A rusted look would appear natural in this type of garden, an effect achieved using Corten steel, expressly devised to take on a crusty texture of oranges and browns. You can see this material used in some outdoor sculptural works as well as cladding on some modern buildings.

Below: *A series of welded steel rings leads the eye directly to the stone circle sculpture.*

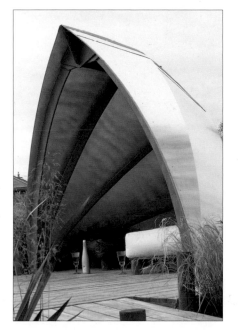

For a homemade alternative, go for a similar effect using heavy steel wire. This is easy to bend and can be built up in several layers to increase the impression of visual weight. Steel reinforcing rods and mesh, normally used in the construction of concrete slabs and walls, are another option, yielding excellent results. All these materials are inexpensive and easy to source.

The circle can be implemented in a number of ways and would make a compelling frame to reveal a secret garden. First divide your space with a solid screen and pierce it with an aperture to encourage the eye to peer through. A single opening works well if the path leads directly towards it, especially if a sculptural object or a specimen tree is revealed beyond. Alternatively, if the path progresses along the wall, a series of apertures could make an interesting walking experience – like a viewing at an art gallery of garden designs.

Left: *A V-shaped, timber-framed structure coated in steel shelters a seating area.*

Paths and Bridges

To make your patio dynamic and interesting, you could include a passage through which you can walk and view the space from different perspectives, perhaps framed by a special entrance. A cabin could be both architecturally intriguing and a refuge or sanctuary in which to escape the stresses of daily life.

Another way to make a passage more of an adventure is to use a bridge in the design. This introduces changes of level and texture and can make a striking architectural feature. Even if there is no existing pond or stream, it can be equally interesting and easy to create a 'dry stream' that is represented by pebbles and rocks and the introduction of appropriate plants among them.

Right: *Sink reclaimed timber planks into a loose surfacing of pebbles.*

Far right: *A bridge of wooden blocks spans this dramatic water sculpture, featuring a wall cascade and formal pool.*

The style of the bridge will depend largely on the level of formality in the garden. A simple, organically styled bridge, suitable for a short span, can be easily created with two or three broad planks of timber. They should be thick enough to avoid twisting and long enough to provide a generous landing on each side of the gap.

Secure them underneath with cross beams to hold them in place and then fix them to posts sunk firmly into concrete foundations below.

Safety around water is an important consideration, so make sure that there is no possibility of movement or settlement. To avoid danger of slipping in wet or icy conditions, fix wire mesh over the surface of the planks.

Where there is a desire for a more sophisticated construction and more of a visual statement, timber and stone bridges offer many attractive possibilities. These would normally be based on classical designs with an arched form to support the bridge, which incidentally creates another circle when reflected in the water below. Practical details, such as steps and handrails, also offer further decorative possibilities.

Small bridges can be purchased off the peg – useful if you are dealing with a small water feature – but where you need to cover a wider span, you will need to commission something made to measure.

Above: *Caged and weathered timbers make an appropriate construction material for furniture in a wild, organic setting.*

Left: *An expressive, free-standing curved timber frame supports a hammock.*

A Sheltered Spot

To complete the calming effect of the contemplative retreat, you can provide a place of shelter, somewhere for meditation or a recreation such as reading and drawing.

You may aspire to a Japanese teahouse and thereby introduce an impressive garden focal point. If possible, site it beside a still pool, with the addition of a wooden deck cantilevered out over the water to bring you as close as possible to nature.

In classic Japanese style, the house would be constructed from beautiful timber posts and cladding, all sanded to a smooth perfection and furnished with a sloping roof and shady veranda. Cover the roof with overlapping wooden shingles instead of tiles and carry rainwater to the ground via delicate brass 'rain chains' in place of downpipes.

A less formal gazebo made of rough timber poles would be a shelter you could create yourself. To give it more of a weightless appearance, build it on a raised wooden platform secured in concrete foundations. Disguise the base structure with a dense perimeter planting of ornamental grasses to suggest a water meadow. Use weatherproof roofing sheets to keep out the rain and cover them inside and out with a simple thatch made from bundles of willows, reeds or brushwood. Ready-made bamboo screening, supplied in rolls, would be adequate to create side walls to give shelter from sun and light breezes, or fill the spaces with a denser screening material, such as wired heather matting.

Furniture should be selected to suit the style of shelter. Seating made from reclaimed timber and sawn planks would be ideal for the rustic gazebo. More formally, choose long, low stone or wooden benches for a traditional 'viewing platform' style of seating.

Above: *This tiny arbour is constructed from oversized square section timbers.*

Above: *A slate plinth creates a relaxing area for viewing and contemplation.*

ORNAMENT AND WATER FEATURES FOR A PEACEFUL SPACE

A serene space needs ornaments that complement the atmosphere and stimulate the senses, with natural forms, soft colours and curving shapes. Water introduces calming, sensory qualities – dancing reflections, shifting shadows and the dreamy sounds of lapping, trickling, spurting or gushing water.

Above: *This display of fish creates a kitsch and amusing touch to a formal pool.*

Simple Approaches

Where space is limited, a modest bowl or container is all that is needed to make an ornamental statement. Borrow ideas for the terrace from tropical Eastern gardens, in which a carefully selected and positioned basin or jar can evoke a sense of perfection and balance. Fill it with water and decorate the surface with floating blooms, or supply a wooden ladle to encourage visitors to refresh themselves on a hot day.

The Sound of the Garden

Introduce sound and movement by attracting birds to the garden. Provide them with a shallow dish with a perching rim and simply take pleasure in watching them bathe. Another idea is bamboo and metal wind chimes, strung from a veranda,

perhaps, or hung in the branches of a tree. These are not only attractive to look at, but they also send out gentle musical notes in even the lightest of breezes.

For something more personal, you can devise your own hanging decorations by stringing together found objects. Drill holes through pebbles, shells and pieces of driftwood to make fascinating and original organic sky sculptures. Rust-stained metal birds and insects associate well with informal gardens and introduce an amusing element when sited among the planting. Oriental-style objects, such as statues of gods and symbolic stone lanterns, make appropriate ornamental statements, while wall plaques extend the decorative possibilities of even the smallest space.

Still Pools

If space permits, then an expanse of water is an asset. You can site a formal pool in an open area untroubled by overhanging trees or shade from boundary walls and buildings. The resulting sheet of cool water will introduce a sense of calm, its surface reflecting light and moving cloudscapes. It creates a quiet place to relax and take in the natural world. The floating leaves of water lilies make ideal landing stages for frogs, pond skaters and dragonflies.

A shallow beach of pebbles bordering a more informal pond encourages wildlife, especially birds, into the water. Plant the edges with marginal moisture-lovers, such as iris, primula and Japanese rush (*Acorus gramineus*), to attract butterflies and other pollinating insects.

Above: *Bamboo wind chimes provide visual and aural texture in the garden.*

Above: *Bronze cranes look at home in this pond, among the giant gunnera leaves.*

Above: *Water bubbles up through a partially opaque Perspex tower.*

Above: *This arrangement of flat pebbles transforms them into an organic sculpture.*

Above: *Water lilies (Nymphaea sp.) won't tolerate running water or fountains.*

Above: *Rocks are used as symbolic mountains in oriental-style gardens.*

This pool could combine with a timber viewing deck, especially if it 'floats' out above the water supported by unseen posts. A canopy would make it a pleasant seating area finished off with a decorative collection of stone jars filled with water-loving grasses, such as papyrus and the graceful, white-spathed arum lily (*Zantedeschia*).

POND PRACTICALITIES

• *Formal water features require a clear area of level ground that is not overshadowed by deciduous trees.*
• *Informal ponds look most natural when they are sited with a background of shrubbery and moisture-loving plants.*
• *Create shallow planting ledges and boggy banks around ponds where planting is required.*
• *Filtration pumps are required for still water displays to keep it free from stagnation and algae.*

Safety note: *Take precautions to prevent children having access to ponds or water features.*

Above: *In this highly stylized, formal water feature, a snaking 'path' of Iris dissects a still pool; select* Iris ensata *'Southern Son', or other moisture-loving species.*

Right: *Cobblestone fountains appear at random throughout this seashore courtyard, bubbling up energetically between the pebbles.*

Moving Water

Where the sounds and textural effects of moving water are wanted, why not introduce a circulating pump into the pool? You can achieve an unusual and energetic effect by arranging the pump outlets so that the water is driven in a circular motion around the margin of the pond. Alternatively, low, gurgling spouts could appear, geyser-like, among a layer of cobbles near the edge of the beach, supplied by a series of small jets from the pump.

A natural-looking cascade would integrate well into an informal pool. Since it is often difficult to dispose of the spoil resulting from the pond excavation, use it to your advantage by creating a hillside. Cover this with a miniature landscape of boulders and rocks, interspersing them with a natural planting of dwarf shrubs, ferns and mosses. Build a water course through the hillside, pump the water up through hidden pipes to the top and then allow it to plunge through to the pool below, where the final delight would be a group of colourful koi carp playing in the eddies.

Taking up much less space than a pond, a gently moving rill would provide an appealing and graphic way to bisect the patio garden. Extra interest can be introduced by pumping the water over a bed of pebbles, in a shallow, snaking channel. More formally, a still, straight canal would provide a neutral, visual resting space between rectangular beds of mono-planted grasses. Line it with a narrow strip of stone or a dark-slate edging to emphasize the contrast between the movement of the plants and the stillness of the dark water.

Above: *A millstone fountain involves drilling through the centre of the stone and concealing a pump below.*

Above: *Pre-formed resin sections can be made up into hillside cascades; infill with bog plants to make them more natural.*

Above: *Cascading rills like these can be incorporated with a new construction, or built into an existing slope.*

INSTALLING A COBBLESTONE FOUNTAIN

The beauty of this type of cobblestone fountain is that it can be situated anywhere in the garden, regardless of whether a body of water exists. All you need is an electricity supply and you can position the fountain at ground level or within a raised bed. Create the gentle bubbling effect of a natural, life-giving spring within a shady meditation corner planted with ferns, hostas and bamboos, or in a more open part of the patio where the upwelling water will sparkle in sunlight and the wet cobbles will gleam. Use gravel, rocks and plants to disguise the electric cable connecting the hidden pump to the waterproof switch.

1 Mark out the diameter of the plastic water reservoir on the ground and dig out a hole slightly wider and deeper than its dimensions. Place a shallow layer of sand at the bottom of the hole and fit the reservoir into the hole.

2 Set the rim level with the surrounding soil and check that it is upright by using a spirit (carpenter's) level across the rim. Lift the reservoir to make any corrections. Backfill the gap with soil, ramming it firmly down with a length of dowel.

3 Place two bricks inside as a plinth for the pump. This prevents the pump's intake becoming clogged with debris. Check that the plastic pipe used for the fountain is high enough to extend up and just through the surface pebbles.

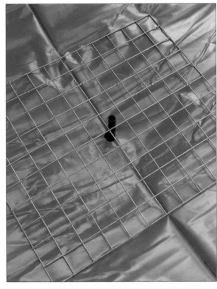

4 Shape the surrounding area into a shallow dish (to direct water back into the reservoir) and cover it and the reservoir with a polythene sheet. Cut a hole in the centre of the plastic to allow the pipe through. Fill the reservoir with water.

5 Check the water flow now in case it needs adjusting. Lay the polythene sheet back over the reservoir with the pipe protruding from the hole. Cover with a piece of rigid galvanized mesh large enough to rest on the rim of the reservoir.

6 Place a smaller mesh over the larger one to catch small pebbles. Add pebbles as necessary to cover the plastic and mesh. Make sure the tip of the delivery pipe is just clear. Connect the cable to a power supply and switch on.

LIGHTING FOR A PEACEFUL SPACE

More than simply fulfilling a practical function, lighting can softly highlight night-time dining areas or draw your focus towards key garden elements – a specimen plant, perhaps, or a Japanese stone lantern. Uplighting bamboos, tree ferns and billowing grasses produces enchantment throughout the year.

Above: *Light simple, coloured glass candleholders along pathways.*

Natural Flame

There's something primal about fire that is utterly captivating. A fire pit could be the central focus of a garden, even in winter, drawing visitors close to stare into the flames and feel the heat. Small, free-tanding circular grates are available, but you could also build a sunken pit lined with firebricks to burn larger logs. In the daytime this could be covered with a decorative metal grid. Ask a local blacksmith to make one for you.

Solid church candles are ideal for use in the garden and they will last longer if you trim the wick after lighting them for the first time. Position them out of draughts – use terracotta pots set among the plants to provide shelter or stand them in wall niches. Small night-lights in coloured glass holders and lanterns also create an inspiring ambiance.

Use night-lights to illuminate a Japanese stone lantern or set them in rugged stone holders along a pathway. Make lighting the candles part of your winding-down ritual.

Modern Technology

The range of solar-powered lights has expanded tremendously and they now burn brighter and more reliably than previously. For the energy conscious, they are a very attractive and versatile alternative to mains powered lights. In some ways, solar-powered lights are more suited to the meditative garden because they follow the natural day-night rhythm and produce a softer effect, but you do need to position them where they can recharge.

New Age lighting effects and light sculptures can be the perfect addition to a meditation garden.

For example, you could use optical-fibre lighting fitted with a unit to create a twinkling starlight effect through decking or paving.

Lights running off a transformer are easy to install, but make sure the transformer has a waterproof housing. You should use a qualified electrician for installing mains-powered lighting.

Small LED spots in white or blue can be used to uplight boulders, large pieces of natural stone and driftwood, revealing the beautiful natural texture and form of these materials. Larger, more architectural plants also benefit from being lit from below and, if you like, these lights can occasionally be fitted with coloured filters. Lights camouflaged as rocks or as shells may also be of use in this type of garden.

Above: *A traditional stone lantern can be lit with an LED or candle.*

Above: *A curved sheet of Perspex creates a water-curtain effect lit by a coloured light.*

Above: *Dichromatic LEDs set into the timbers provide atmospheric lighting.*

Lighting Water

Since water plays a major role in patios designed to soothe, it makes sense to highlight these features at night. On a still, reflecting pool you could float candles, purpose-made oil lamps or clear electric globes that bob on the surface. Underwater pool lighting should be understated so that it does not interfere with the reflections of the night sky. If you use coloured light, pick one shade, such as a deep blue. Light oriental-style bridges to reveal their arcing shapes using tiny camouflaged LED spots or hang candle lanterns to light the way.

Cascades are best lit from below; in a terraced courtyard you could combine a water curtain falling over a sheet of transparent Perspex (Plexiglass) with gradually changing coloured light.

Above: *This pool has an integral abstract sculpture made of tall bamboo poles. The artistic lighting system transforms it into a dream landscape.*

LIGHTING PLANTS WITH UPLIGHTERS

Intriguing patterns and atmospheric effects can be created using low-voltage LED spotlights as uplighters. These spotlights run off a transformer and are variously positioned around the plants and pots to give different effects. In the set used here there are two spots with contemporary brushed-steel casings and optional wall brackets or ground spikes. When they are hidden among the foliage of pot plants or in a border you hardly notice them at all during the day. It is safer and more practical if you can switch the lights on and off from a convenient point indoors or from a shelter or retreat within the patio.

1 The lights are fixed into the containers by pushing the ground spike down into the compost (soil mix). The arrangement of differently sized pots gives more scope for experimenting with various effects, with spots set to give a combination of up- and down-lighting.

2 Fixing the lights behind a fern throws its fronds into relief. You can also shine one of the lights on to the wall behind to give more of a sense of depth and separation and, in this case, by glimpsing some of the purple wall colour you help to create a relaxing ambiance.

3 LED lights produce virtually no heat when they are on, so you don't have to worry about scorching your plant foliage. Here the potted sedge in the foreground looks almost like an optical fibre lamp popular in the 1960s with the light shining though its fine strands.

MODERN SPACES

The architecture of our living spaces should provide an antidote to the pressures of modern life. The contemporary patio, with its clean lines and low-maintenance approach, should have the same effect: a clear, uncluttered and relaxing perspective.

Hard landscaping plays a significant role in modern exterior design and the range of new materials available has changed many preconceptions about garden style. Industrial materials, such as stainless steel and concrete, are finding new uses in the garden, as are coloured Perspex, glass and 'intelligent' textiles.

The contemporary patio is an excellent vehicle to showcase avant-garde design, using clean backdrops and screens against which to display modern sculpture, dramatic water features and three-dimensional planting. It makes a stimulating setting for entertaining, a place to show off exciting forms of modern outdoor furniture, and has many possibilities for special lighting and sound effects.

Left: *This striking design uses strong colour contrasts and bold geometry. Coloured aggregates are used as decorative mulches – combined in this way they create a strong visual impression of three-dimensional form, from what is actually a flat surface.*

FLOORING FOR A MODERN SPACE

Your hard-landscaping choices can reflect the naturally occurring materials in your region. Alternatively, you can create a wild fantasy of unexpected colours, textures and materials. Clean lines and bold statements sum up the image of contemporary outdoor design, and flooring provides the first and most fundamental way to set the scene.

Above: *Grey slate highlights the turning corner of steps from the sandstone path.*

Left: *Grass is attractive but can be slippery and prone to wear. Square concrete paving slabs provide a secure walking surface and an attractive pattern.*

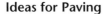

Straight grids of slabs will produce the most tailored effect. However, while a design of squares may work in small spaces, it may be monotonous over a larger area. Rectangles usually have a more sympathetic appearance and can help create an illusion of width or length where this is required. They tend to offer a better sense of movement and are normally used as identical-sized elements in a staggered pattern. Alternatively, they may be cut in random lengths, but in widths that are identical, or in no more than three varying widths to add interest and directional movement.

Ideas for Paving

Paving offers a wide choice of materials, colours and finishes. Natural stone slabs tend to offer the most elegant solution for a formal design, with a wide variety of tones and textures from which to choose.

Pale-coloured limestone is a popular choice for modern designs, especially in an urban location where its cool tones and light-reflecting qualities introduce calm and luminosity. It also has a fairly uncompromising look, so if you want something gentler, sandstone provides honey and golden hues. Slate has subtle variations of green, grey and plum, but may also be golden and fiery. Natural stone varies enormously in colour and texture.

It is tempting to order materials online, but it is always preferable to handle, examine and compare physical samples before purchasing. With so many products available, it is helpful to understand the differences in texture and colour. UK and European stone tends to be subtle in tone and texture, while material deriving from Africa, India and China can have a more fiery look.

The method by which the stone is cut and finished will alter the look of the paving scheme as well. Sawn slabs with crisp edges and a smooth surface are ideal for a modern style. The shape of the slab and the laying pattern are important, too: bold floor patterns will help to give the paving a crisp, clean appearance.

Above: *Stepping-stones of smooth sawn sandstone make a crisp, bridging pathway.*

LAYING PAVING SLABS

Neatly finished and perfectly level paving, using either square or rectangular units, is likely to be a major surfacing component in the modern patio. The choice of materials is personal and dependent on the specific style, but relatively plain, crisply finished slabs of either sawn natural stone, split slate, or concrete work well.

1 Excavate to a depth that allows for about 5cm (2in) of compacted hardcore or rubble topped with 5cm (2in) of ballast (sand and gravel), plus the thickness of the paving.

2 Place five blobs of mortar on the hardcore, one in the centre, the others near the corners. Bed the slab on the mortar, check it is level and tap with a rubber mallet to correct.

3 If creating a large area, lay slabs on a slight slope to ensure efficient drainage. Continue to lay the paving slabs on the mortar, until you have covered the whole area.

4 Space the slabs with pegs. After a couple of days, mortar the joints using a dryish mortar mix and a trowel, pushing it well down. Recess the mortar slightly.

Juxtapositions

Paths, steps and terraces can benefit from contrasting details to highlight elements. These do not have to be complicated: a dark-toned detail using slate or granite, combined with a pale limestone would give a sharp result, while an edging of honeyed sandstone produces a contrast that reinforces the design more subtly.

The use of plant material in conjunction with paving slabs will also produce a softening effect. Low-growing herbs in place of regular jointing would enliven a terrace; position slabs far enough apart to allow space for the planting. Alternatively, arrange square slabs in a grid pattern to make a formal, chequered design in a grass lawn.

There are many good examples of economy paving products, such as those made from tinted concrete or reconstituted stone dust formed in moulds taken from natural products. To stay in line with the contemporary concept, choose simple designs with a natural finish and colour.

Right: *A daisy floor pattern is achieved with contrasting cream and black setts.*

Left: *An agave with diminutive grey succulents and drought-resistant herbs help to animate this surreal desert landscape of crushed turquoise-coloured shells.*

laid on the surface after pouring. The surplus cement is then brushed off before it has completely dried to expose the granular material.

To prepare the ground area for concrete, it must be levelled and laid with a compressed hardcore foundation. The form and layout of the design is then set out using bands of shuttering material, such as marine ply. The concrete cement mix is poured in, tamped down to push out air, and then allowed to cure and set. For making steps and small areas of paving, concrete is poured into moulds formed on site using a system of shuttering to hold the shape in place. This is potentially a self-build project, as the system is economic and easy to create yourself with the aid of a cement mixer and levelling tools.

Creative Additions

Unusual and unexpected materials are frequently utilized as part of modern garden design. Coloured aggregates in the form of crushed glass, for example, and tinted stone chippings can play interesting roles

Detailing and Relief

Manufactured shapes are also made solely to add detailing to an area of paving such as edging. Ammonite and split-cobble forms, for example, can introduce an interesting relief to a plain design, especially effective when it is used in conjunction with a water feature or sculptural object. They might be introduced effectively in a sinuous, snaking line carefully cut through paving, or laid through a background of grass or contrasting stone chippings.

Poured concrete offers interesting solutions for paving and steps and it is the material to choose if you are looking for an absolutely smooth, clear surface. Pure white cement makes a more refreshing alternative to the normal grey, or coloured pigments may be added to the mix to make a bold contrast statement.

Specialists now offer concrete with a polished surface that brings a super level of cool sophistication to a modern scheme. If you are looking for a more textured effect, then aggregates such as polished pebbles or coloured glass nuggets can be incorporated into the mix or

Right: *Concrete replica ammonites provide relief detail in this paving scheme.*

in flooring, for mulches and as decorative panels. They can be arranged in an infinite array of different designs and can be used to make up tantalizing geometric *trompe l'oeil* effects or chequered grids to create coloured 'set-piece' beds in place of traditional planting. They also lend themselves to more fluid, curvaceous shapes that might be incorporated with a scheme of tapestry-planting.

Granules of recycled rubber can surface pathways or be used in place of vegetative, moisture-retaining mulch. As well as neutral black, this material is available in many bright colours; because of its soft, rubbery qualities it is ideal for making up into animated designs suitable for children's play areas.

Futuristic Materials

Industrial steel grid panels are normally used for making steps and high-level decks, but they can also be used for ground-level paths. To achieve a minimalist effect, try setting them over natural gravel or coloured aggregate to create a startling contrast. Even more spectacularly, create a dramatic

Above: *Industrial steel mesh panels create paths across an area of tapestry planting.*

design feature by floating the grid panels over an area planted with diminutive succulent plants and ferns, to show off the foliage below. This creates a practical pathway, in this case to allow access for a car, that combines and contrasts geometric pattern with organic texture.

Solid sheet metal offers an alternative look for flooring. Stainless or anodized steel brings

Above: *Green astroturf has a luminous quality, offset by the stark screen walls.*

a sharp, edgy look to a crisp design scheme and it can be finished with a studded surface that is attractive and will also help to reduce slipping. Panels of this material are especially suited to being used as raised pathways or decks, perhaps over a water feature, or to span two separate parts of the garden.

Although functional, metal becomes hot to the touch in the sun and slippery in the wet – so you will need to exercise discretion in its use.

Often, timber planking can be used in place of metal to achieve the same objective, and this is especially suited to pool decking. Wood also lends a warm, organic feel to the garden and it is normally more practical. High-quality hardwoods such as maple, birch and ash are the best to choose, as they are more able to stand up to the rigours of heat, cold and wet. Make sure you use sustainable sources for hardwood. Alternatively, use naturally durable soft woods such as Western red cedar, Southern yellow pine, white fir or heavy planks of pressure-treated pine.

Above: *Splayed bands of timber accentuate the curves of this gravel path.*

Above: *This cube illusion is achieved with rectangles of glass and stone chippings.*

WALLS AND SCREENS FOR A MODERN SPACE

Solid backdrops in the form of enclosing walls and screens can help to create an uncluttered setting for a formal modern patio. Concrete is probably the most versatile building material, but eye-catching solutions can also be achieved using metal, glass, stone and wood in an imaginative way.

Above: *A solid screen wall benefits from a large opening to view the garden beyond.*

Adaptable Concrete

Concrete is a superb material for a range of applications, from making the retaining walls for raised planting beds to the creation of formal, above-ground pools and water features. It can also be made into free-standing screens and other garden design features.

A solid screen could be incorporated into a water cascade, or it could function as a stand-alone backdrop to a piece of sculpture or artwork. In addition, a concrete screen makes an ideal support for lighting, with the wiring hidden out of sight inside, for special night-time effects.

As good as they are for creating privacy from neighbours, solid screens and boundary walls can be overpowering at times. When

Above: *Small, quirky details can do a lot to relieve a monotonous run of walling; colour-co-ordinated pots and a timber beam finish the opening effectively.*

Above: *These bold timber columns create a screen without closing off the garden.*

Above: *This wall of staggered wooden blocks achieves enormous textural interest.*

pierced with portholes or windows, however, their bulk is relieved and, where appropriate, you can benefit from views to the other side.

Concrete can be poured into shuttering moulds to create very elegant vertical features, but the more usual, and economical, method is to construct the wall with concrete building blocks, strengthened with reinforcing rods. A cement render is then applied to give the wall a smooth, even finish. For a permanent colour finish, incorporate special tinting pigments into the render; otherwise, you can use an exterior paint once the cement has completely dried. Stunning polished concrete effects can also be achieved in the hands of specialists.

CREATING A BOLD CANVAS

Depending on the colour you choose, a painted wall can act like a giant canvas hanging in your outdoor room. If selected with care, colour will add energy to a space, especially one used for entertaining, and either become a focal point in its own right or make a stunning backdrop to the patio. Before committing to a colour, use a sample to paint a small square area of heavy paper and view in position.

1 Begin by clearing a space around the wall so that you can work in relative comfort. Check that the rendering is sound and make any repairs before starting work. If it has never been painted before, seal the surface of the render with a PVA solution and allow it to dry.

2 If the render has been previously painted, prepare the surface for repainting by brushing it down with a soft-bristled hand brush to remove cobwebs and any debris, especially in corners and under the coping stones. Use a scraper and wire brush on painted brick to lift loose paint.

3 Having followed the manufacturer's instructions for preparing the paint, stirring it as directed, begin by applying a coat of paint to the edges using a small brush. Exterior-quality paints, including masonry paint, can be custom-coloured to match any colour sample.

4 Continue to work around the edges of the wall taking care to protect the flooring with a tarpaulin, dust sheets or plastic sheeting – it can be very time consuming to remove paint splashes, especially from textured surfaces. Use a smaller brush still for any narrow strips.

5 To paint the remaining central area of render, switch to a large brush or roller. Particularly with strong or deep shades, you may notice that the surface appears patchy as it dries. Leave it for the required amount of drying time, which varies depending on the temperature.

6 Once the first coat of paint is dry, apply the second, using the same technique. You may even need a little touching up after that. Comparing this scene with the first, you can see how dramatic the space has become. Add a finishing touch with the container plants and furniture.

Left: *This design relies on illusion and colour. Panels of Perspex form the backdrop to a rectilinear layout of beds. Three* Ligustrum delavayanum *stand sentinel.*

Transparency and Colour

Glass is a superb screening material, able to block the wind without obscuring the view – an important feature for riverside and high-level terraces. Glass bricks can be useful in all or part of a boundary wall, to admit light with no loss of privacy.

Mirrored glass offers an illusory role, reflecting light into a shady area or multiplying images to give a false idea of space and dimension. It can be set into a wall to reflect an interesting feature or the façade opposite to create a double image. More inventively, a series of free-standing mirror screens set among low planting will reflect endless repeating images of foliage and skyscape to fantastic visual effect.

Colour produces a surreal effect in translucent materials, its intensity changing throughout the day as the lighting conditions vary. Coloured glass is especially suited to modern, stained-glass windows, providing relief and sculptural interest when set into a plain wall.

Alternatively, Perspex (Plexiglass) offers a tough, lightweight solution and is easier to handle and fix, so is attractive for large-scale applications.

A group of screens made in dazzling primary colours would make a striking sculptural statement; a single large screen composed of coloured panels could take on the look of a Mondrian painting, while throwing an evocative colour cast across its surroundings as light passes through it.

Light and Shine

Stainless steel can be polished to a mirror-like shine that will throw back light while creating interesting,

Above: *An ephemeral screen uses clear Perspex floats strung on nylon cord.*

distorted reflections of planting or decorative objects beside it. It makes an excellent screening material for boundaries and backdrops, and it is especially useful for introducing an extra sense of dimension or for lighting up a shady area.

Steel sheets can be used in a solid mass where it is desirable to block a view or create a special effect. For partial screening, where you want a hint of the view beyond, intricate designs can be cut out using a laser.

Steel offers other solutions for semi-opaque screening. Industrial wire mesh provides the means to separate areas of the garden, or to make boundary enclosures that do not completely block a view. Rigid panels can be easily made by fixing the mesh in wooden frames, which can be screwed into timber posts set in the ground. Alternatively, it is possible to obtain stainless steel in sheet form with geometric perforations that produce a delicate relief. This produces an elegant solution for smaller, detailed effects within a screen.

Above: *A curvaceous, stainless-steel screen makes an arresting modern backdrop.*

A MODERN PERGOLA

Using a basic pergola kit or self-build framework as a foundation (see page 95 for step-by-step construction), you can customize a pergola to create a feature that is more in keeping with the architecture and overall design theme of a contemporary patio. Traditional trellis panels don't always sit well against a modern backdrop, so you should explore other screening materials. These might include translucent or coloured panels of Perspex (Plexiglass) such as the ones used below. Alternatively, consider metal-framed units of lashed technical fabric.

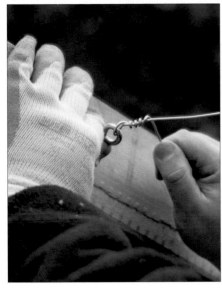

1 Using wooden crossbeams can give a pergola a heavy, weighty feel and make the overall structure look more traditional, or even rustic. As an alternative to this, screw in metal vine eyes and attach galvanized training wire. Secure the wire to the eyes and tighten.

2 Once they are all in place, the taut galvanized training wires form a versatile, lightweight 'roof' for the framework of the pergola. These wires are well able to support a tracery of climbing plants, outdoor lights or some form of temporary sun screening, such as a sail.

3 Coloured surfaces play more of a role in the modern patio garden, so you may want to paint the woodwork using an outdoor-quality paint. A small roller and paint tray make this a quick and easy task. Avoid overloading the roller and cover the ground to catch splashes.

4 To attach Perspex or Plexiglass prefabricated screens, drill holes at regular intervals through the frame and into the pergola's supporting timber upright and then secure the screen in position with galvanized screws.

5 To support the other side of the screen, either attach it to another pergola upright or fix a shorter post into the ground – which will be hidden behind the screen – and attach the frame of the screen to that.

6 The arrangement of screens shown here allows multiple entrances and exits to the patio area beneath the pergola, keeping the structure feeling airy and spacious. The floor is gravel laid over consolidated hardcore.

PLANTS AND CONTAINERS FOR A MODERN SPACE

Geometry and scale are important design factors. In a minimalist design, all the bones are laid bare so the planting must play more than a supporting role. Clean architectural lines depend heavily on planting statements to introduce an organic equilibrium with the hard elements.

Above: *Architectural plants like this arum lily (Zantedeschia) make a bold statement.*

Left: *This ebullient architectural planting uses spiky foliage specimens that include palms, cycads and mature bear grass (Dasylirion serratifolium).*

Planting Choices

Bold planting statements are necessary in a contemporary garden, and structured blocks of single-species monoplanting help to achieve the right balance of weight and scale. They can aid a sense of progression through a space by means of sequential repetition or create focal points and special features.

The passage of a broad, uncluttered terrace or pathway can be reinforced by judicious planting choices. Trees trained with bare trunks to eye height and topped with a mop-head canopy make interesting vertical statements. Plant them in line, 3m (10ft) or so apart, on either side of a terrace to create a walkway. Underplant each specimen with a block of shrubs to give a sense of visual weight at ground level. This can be achieved by depending entirely on evergreens to have a permanent year-round presence. Holly (*Ilex* sp.), Portuguese laurel (*Prunus lusitanica*) and *Elaeagnus x ebbingei* make good tree subjects. They all have the necessary height and the ability to tolerate regular trimming. *Buxus* and *Ligustrum* work well to make the cubes below, while green ivy will create a tight ground cover that is easy to maintain.

Trees and Shrubs

Although deciduous trees drop their leaves in winter, they have the advantage of changing foliage colour throughout the year, so altering the appearance of the garden season by season. Some have other special qualities, as they take well to forming and training, especially in a method known as 'pleaching'. Here the canopy is trained on horizontal wires eventually to produce a long, unbroken block of foliage above head height, with the bare trunks showing beneath.

This rather grand style is particularly suitable for defining boundaries – either to reinforce a pathway, for example, or to frame a feature such as a pool or seating area. Lime (*Tilia*) is frequently used for its pale green leaves and scented summer flowers. However, hornbeam (*Carpinus betulus*) retains its rich, brown autumn foliage for a long time, adding an extra dimension in winter. It is useful for structural work, as it can be trained into hedges, archways and columns.

Above: *The bleached white trunks of silver birch trees frame low-growing box balls.*

HOW TO PRUNE BAMBOO

The grace and beauty of bamboo tends to diminish unless established plants are pruned annually. The aim is to be able to admire the line, colour and markings of the stems, or culms, by reducing congestion and removing debris. You can also control the spread of more invasive types by removing emerging shoots.

1 Cut out a proportion of the oldest stems at ground level. Those more than three years old tend to have dense whorls of leafy branches. In addition, take out some of the thinnest, weakest stems.

2 Avoid leaving short stumps of stems after pruning, as these go hard and take a long time to rot. Pull out any dead, rotted stems. A lot of dead stems may mean that the plant is dying after flowering.

3 Cut out any dead stems at the base as well as dead side shoots. Also remove stems that are crossing upright stems. Cut off the lower side shoots as close to the main stem as possible.

4 Leave the leaf litter at the base of the bamboo to allow the silica bound up in the dead leaves to be recycled. Apply a mulch of bulky organic matter in early spring to feed plants.

Small shrubs, such as fragrant, silvery *Santolina* and lavender, respond well to clipping into low, tight shapes suitable for edges and underplanting, but even better, they make excellent subjects for geometric tapestry designs. Taller-growing yew (*Taxus baccata*) and box (*Buxus sempervirens*) make good, dark evergreen subjects with excellent screening possibilities.

You can clip them into neat, rectangular blocks or rounded balls and spheres of foliage, which can be laid out in rows within a precise geometric template.

Low-growing bamboos also lend themselves to block planting and barrier edging; white-striped *Pleioblastus variegatus* and white-edged *Sasa veitchii* are both excellent candidates for this treatment.

Textural Planting

It is possible to create a range of adventurous optical effects that echo the architectural features of the patio design. Chequerboard and striped effects work well for tapestry planting when they can be easily viewed from above. Taller plants, used in regularly repeated patterns, can be employed to create screens and borders for paths. For low-level work, mat-spreading, mound- or tuft-forming evergreens make the best choice. Contrasting colours help to accentuate the display, with combinations of grey and lime, purple and black being extremely effective.

Interesting texture plays an important role. The black, blade-like foliage of *Ophiopogon planiscapus* 'Nigrescens' makes a gleaming and faintly sinister statement. In contrast, the needle-fine, grey-tufted grass *Festuca glauca* has a light and airy elegance. Ground-hugging succulents can be used to provide an exotic textural effect; the rosette-forming *Sempervivum* group and some of the hardy sedums are ideal.

Above: *White iris and frothy gypsophila complement this cool architectural design.*

Above: *Swathes of mono-planting add texture and movement.*

The colours of sedum, which vary from silver-grey through to reddish-purple, can be set off beautifully by a contrasting mineral mulch. White marble chippings, mauve slate and dark, polished river pebbles lend a sophisticated touch; by contrast coloured materials, such as crushed glass and plastics, can produce living pop-art displays.

Dynamics of Contrast

A tropical planting treatment can act as a foil to the cool, clean lines of contemporary architecture, introducing an energetic visual experience composed of exotic flowers, spiky leaves and tall, textured trunks. Palm trees, agaves and yuccas, phormium and cordyline, all have the architectural strength required to hold their own against a stark backdrop of bare walls and floors. A large specimen can be used singly to make a big, bold statement, though strong planting groups will create an exhilarating theatre of shape and form. Their sunlit shadows will dance by day, while judicious uplighting at night will throw their dramatic silhouettes in bizarre patterns against walls, screens and floors.

Containers for Planting

A patio garden can be dependent on containers, largely due to restricted space or lack of available ground for planting. In high-level projects, such as balconies and roof terraces, all the planting has, of necessity, to be in containers, either free-standing or built in. This is a high-maintenance form of gardening, requiring excellent soil quality, fastidious preparation and a very regular watering regime.

To complement the pared-down, minimalist style, planting containers should also be clean-lined and possess a bold, sculptural integrity. New shapes tend to have tall, narrower proportions than traditional pots, although still normally retaining a round or square shape. These forms work especially well when arranged in straight-lined groups, producing an elegant, sequential statement, to create a geometric backdrop or to line a pathway. Matching pairs can be used to frame a doorway or entrance, or mark a descent of steps. They do have one drawback, however; the height combined with a narrow base makes them unstable in exposed, windy sites and where children may be playing.

Above: *Bold green planting animates the soft grey of these weathered zinc containers.*

Cubes and wider, curved shapes are the solution to this problem. These offer potentially greater planting possibilities, too. The unusual height of a tall, slim pot must be balanced by squat planting to retain stability – an evergreen ball or cube of box, for example. Broad shapes in large sizes have the physical and visual volume to support a decent shrub or small tree, with their greater need for soil and root capacity.

Materials play an important role of course, and they should reflect and balance the ambiance of the hard landscaping. Terracotta, with its excellent cultural qualities, is the traditional material for plant pots. Its style has moved on over the centuries, however. The newest look uses white, grey or taupe-coloured clay to produce simple, but oversized containers with enormous integrity and elegance. The flat, matt finish ties in beautifully with both natural wood and the painted exterior joinery.

Glazed finishes offer an alternative look with the potential of a range of soft colours, but bear in mind that only stoneware (not terracotta) is suitable where there is a danger of frost.

Above: *A block planting of single species with co-ordinated colours.*

Above: *This large weathered pot is surrounded by tropical ferns and planting.*

Right: *The containers here include rectangular galvanized planters, a black metal planter and vintage zinc dolly bins.*

Plastics offer the ideal solution where striking appearance and bold colour are required. Moulded containers in PVC, resins and fibreglass offer a variety of styles and sizes suited to very modern, extreme designs. Some are in shiny primary colours, up to 2m (6½ft) tall, and are sculptures in their own right. Others are more subdued – cubes and bowls in matt, translucent finishes that can even be adapted to lighting features.

Apart from their visual qualities, the huge advantage of these containers is their lightness – they are easy to handle and perfectly suited to roof gardens and balconies.

Zinc offers another lightweight container solution, with graciously elegant modern forms that retain a classic twist. Pure, round, classic shapes work in all situations, while cubes and tall rectangles can be juggled together to form an intriguing plant jigsaw. The best types are acid treated to a sober, dark finish and double-skinned, to keep the root-ball (roots) protected from heat. This look mixes well with crisp designs in pale timber decking and cool limestone paving.

Oversized round and rectangular timber plant containers have a real contemporary edge. Made from European oak or tropical hardwood, they are an excellent foil for a garden dependent on darker stone surfaces.

POTTING UP A SEDGE

Grasses and evergreen sedges (*Carex*), as well as other plants with narrow, linear foliage, have the right look for modern outdoor spaces. Many require a minimum of maintenance and have an airy, space-saving habit. Covering the compost (soil mix) with a sparkling and colourful decorative mulch adds to the contemporary feel.

1 Cover the drainage hole with a piece of tile or crock and pour 4–5cm (1½–2in) of gravel into the base. Cover the gravel with a little loam-based compost (soil mix). Soak the plant in its pot to wet the root-ball (roots).

2 Remove the plastic pot and try the sedge (here *Carex* 'Prairie Fire') for size. The finished compost level should be the same as the original nursery level, but leave space for a layer of mulch and for water to pool on top.

3 Gathering up the foliage of the sedge at the base, work in more compost to fill the gap around the root-ball. Check that there are no large air spaces by using your fingers to feed compost further down and firm lightly.

4 Choose a mulch of coloured glass chippings or acrylic chips. Work the chips around the base of the plant, covering the compost thoroughly. The finished plant should be watered well and stood in a bright or partially shaded site.

STRUCTURES FOR A MODERN SPACE

The contemporary garden is an opportunity to use materials in new and unexpected ways. Three-dimensional structures within an outdoor space, such as an arch or a shelter, tend to loosely follow conventional approaches, but are interpreted in ways where the materials, execution, design and visual impact are more prominent than the purpose.

Above: *These curvaceous screens bring a new dimension to willow weaving.*

Left: *A tall screen strung with interwoven wires brings a sense of enclosure to one of a series of circular terraces on a sloping site, all enclosed by curving walls.*

Establishing the Structures
Vertical elements add a crucial dimension to every garden design, introducing perspective and contrast between the planting and the house. These vertical elements may be purely symbolic in nature, or they could provide practical roles of shelter and retreat.

Spatial divisions provide an effective way to introduce focus, while creating real or illusory visual separations between different areas of the garden. Free-standing, vertical posts offer a host of opportunities to create impressive visual effects in a really simple way, by arresting the eye without affecting the overall view.

Install the posts in single rows to make a partition or backdrop, or double them up to accentuate a pathway and organize directional flow so that the garden unfolds to visitors as you would wish it to be seen. Alternatively, they can be arranged in straight lines, grids, waves, curves or circles depending on the effect you want to create.

Construction and Finish
You can choose any vertical layout to suit your design format, but the construction material and finish will differentiate one concept of garden from another. A cool, architectural style would normally call for crisp, engineered materials, such as stainless steel or aluminium. In this case, posts would be formed from slim rods or hollow tubing. Metal with a rusted appearance provides a more organic look and one that is easier to produce at home.

Reinforcing rods used in concrete construction once more have a role to play. You can create a screen wall of vertical rods using a heavy wooden beam set on the ground – simply drill holes at 2–4cm (¾–1½in) intervals and push the metal rods in firmly. The rods might all finish on a single horizontal plane, or you can cut them into different heights to produce a wave effect. Stiff wire or even plastic rods could be used instead for a more ephemeral effect.

Wire and plastic mesh are versatile materials to incorporate into a semi-opaque structure. To create an intriguing feature, build a framework in the form of a

Above: *This sweeping tunnel is formed from hoops of thin plastic film.*

rectilinear cage, fixing the mesh all around it and on top. This would make an effective statement on its own, but an extra dimension could be achieved by the addition of a spreading deciduous shrub, such as *Cotoneaster dammeri*. During construction, plant the shrub on the inside of the structure, so that the framework of stems can be seen in winter.

Reinterpreting Traditional Materials

Wood is readily available and can be worked with the type of tools found in the home workshop. Timber posts have seemingly endless possibilities; arranged in groups, they provide an unusual way to create a simple and effective sculptural feature. It would be easy to create features for an organic-style design using bold, square timber sections from a sawmill, or you may be able to source the round poles used for supporting telephone wires. To introduce different textural effects, try

Above: *This futuristic raised terrace has satellite seating and an overhead shelter.*

wrapping them in heavy rope, perhaps leaving tassels to drift in the breeze. Try a contemporary swag effect, taking a closely banded series of taut ropes, passed through holes drilled in the uprights.

Another option is to make a pergola, attaching horizontal rails above head height. The pergola can be fixed to the house or a garden cabin, or build it as a free-standing structure over a pathway to draw the eye and emphasize a route.

A structure of bold posts and rails will cast shadows that change shape and direction as the sun passes across the sky, so adding to the dynamic effect of the arrangement. A roof of mesh material would offer a different strategy, providing structural support for climbing plants and a fixing point for lighting.

Metal elements can be combined with timber to alter the weight or style of the structure. Multi-stranded steel wire is immensely strong, but visually extremely light; it can be tensioned vertically or horizontally and then incorporated into a pergola structure, railings, gates or even screen doors.

Steel reinforcing mesh would offer the same structural function, but with an industrial and less elegant finish. Large sheets of this heavy, rigid mesh can be fixed flat to create a 'window' feature for a cabin wall, or it could be curved – perhaps to achieve a tunnel to support informal climbing plants.

A cabin is a desirable feature if there is space, offering a three-dimensional visual statement while providing the important features of shade, shelter and storage.

The structure may echo some architectural features of the house, or be created in free form, to accentuate the layout of the ground plan, for example. The style can be anything from hi-tech gleaming steel and glass to a low-key timber construction. The incorporation of a solid roofed veranda would provide shade from sun and shelter from light rain, making an ideal place for a viewing terrace to admire the garden. This would of course call for comfortable furniture as the location encourages lounging. It could also create a perfect place for a dining space.

FURNITURE FOR A MODERN SPACE

Having planned the structural elements, you should now have a sheltered spot for your seating area. Don't choose 'modern' furniture just for the sake of it – select it to fit comfortably with the decisions you've already made. So look at the options available using both established and experimental materials – from wood and aluminium to concrete and plastic.

Above: *This moulded organic, free-form seat creates a striking sculptural form.*

Left: *An immaculately detailed bench and table system has been incorporated with the construction of this patio.*

Perhaps the most exciting recent development is a stranded plastic, which can be woven like basketware. Elegant and functional and, as a bonus, comfortable too.

Inviting, weather-resistant, outdoor furniture is available at last. Deep sofas and armchairs with matching occasional tables bring five-star hotel style to the home. For the ultimate luxury, choose a wonderfully sensual, circular double lounger, complete with a curvaceous, lidded canopy. A perfect hideaway.

At the opposite extreme, and following current trends in new uses for materials, furniture made from concrete is now available.

Material Options

Wood is the traditional material for exterior furniture and always looks at home in the garden. However, new designs incorporate other materials to give an edgier, lighter appearance, more akin to interior furniture and well suited to a crisp, modern garden terrace.

Aluminium frames, stone and slate tabletops and textile seats feature frequently. Moulded plastics in bright, pop colours offer comfortable and practical new-look seating. Lightweight and easy to store, a set of pink or lime-green chairs with a matching café table would introduce a cheerful note to a balcony or terrace.

Above: *A slab of limestone has been sculpted into a stunning feature bench.*

Above: *Translucent materials like glass and plastic make the most of the available light.*

Sometimes more functional than comfortable, it can, nevertheless, be found in organic forms that add an interesting sculptural feature to the patio. Polished finishes help to make the look attractive; concrete

Above: *Armchairs of woven stranded plastic are lightweight and weather resistant.*

can even be used for dining furniture, and the incorporation of fibre optics in the table surface will undoubtedly add drama to an evening's entertainment.

Creating Shelter

Shade from the summer sun is an important consideration for eating areas, and an overhead canopy is probably the most attractive solution where space allows. Where practical, these can be fixed to a convenient wall, but a free-standing model is another option. The most beautiful resemble curvy, floating sails, restrained by cables to the ground, creating an ephemeral sculptural statement in a modern garden setting. They may be made from canvas or from one of the innovative intelligent textiles that deflect the hot sun. Alternatively, a gazebo-style canopy makes a good semi-permanent solution that can be easily taken down and stored

Above: *Simple treatments yield big results. A long curving bench encloses this roof terrace, with folding chairs and a low table creating an intimate seating area.*

over winter. Washable textiles and integral curtains make these an appealing choice when a permanent structure is not feasible.

Parasols can be quickly erected wherever the need arises, but to be effective the canopy should be large and this tends to make them heavy and unmanageable.

Oversized shades with aluminium frames and winding devices are a practical choice, especially when fixed permanently to the ground. The best can be orientated according to the position of the sun, avoiding the need to move them about. Summertime lunch can then become a pleasurable experience, while evenings can be illuminated by lighting strings incorporated into the frame.

ORNAMENT FOR A MODERN SPACE

The clean, cool space of a modern patio can be seen as an outdoor gallery, providing a theatrical context for contemporary sculpture. A terrace may provide only enough space to display a single statement piece of work, while a larger courtyard garden could stage a varied collection of different sculptural elements, or a large installation that dominates the whole area.

Above: *A decorative spiral of recycled, crushed windscreen glass.*

Modern Displays

Outside, flooded with natural light, the texture of a decorative piece alters from an interior display. Another interesting relationship is how ornamental elements link to a landscape with shrubs and trees. A piece of stone, when carved and polished, becomes an evocative and sensual form, and by exposing its ancient strata lines and colour a connection is made between the rock and its natural origins.

Wood, too, has a powerful connection with the natural world. Once rooted in the earth, it now gives up its innermost secrets to the artist's chisel or saw. Or, suggesting a period of prehistory, an ancient root burr might stand alone, its unworked, natural form interpreted as a piece of abstract sculpture.

Above: *This dramatic metal sculpture is enclosed by a curved, free-standing wall.*

Above: *Glass slivers in a curling framework of steel wire create an ephemeral effect.*

Above: *This humorous Mediterranean-style feature suggests both pool and boules – water not required.*

A construction that is formed from strands of wire has the effect of being just light and air; it seems to drift on the breeze, a gossamer vision to be caught only by chance. Mirrored glass possesses similarly elusive qualities and can be used to clever effect by multiplying images to present a constantly changing series of views to the onlooker. A group of tall, free-standing mirror panels might form the central focus to a patio, catching the skyscape by day, but appearing ghostly by night with subtle moonlit effects.

WATER FOR A MODERN SPACE

Water is an important element of a contemporary patio. As well as providing calm and serenity, it animates a space and offers exciting sculptural possibilities. Much of the emphasis of garden design in recent years has been on innovative water features – spinning crystal orbs vying with shimmering towers of glass or pyramids of bright steel.

Above: *The finest vertical jets of water bisect a brilliant circle of tubular steel.*

Tumbling Water

The tumbling cascade has long inspired the imagination of the gardening world. You may lack the space to having a swimming pool on a terrace, but this is an easy technique to adapt as either a built-in or free-standing feature.

In terms of space, all you require for a cascade is simply a small, formal reservoir pool backed by a narrow wall. This is furnished with a simple spout or wide slot for the water to emerge through, which is pumped up from below.

A forceful cascade will break up the pool surface, creating dancing light and shadow. Another option is to fill the pool space with a bed of glass pebbles and light them from below to create a night-time glow.

Above: *This elegant cascade allows water to slip slowly overboard to a larger pool below. The upper ledge offers a good perching spot – conveniently beside the wine cooler.*

Above: *This low-key feature really proves that less can be more.*

Above: *Carefully organized chutes let water slip down gently from one to the next.*

Wall of Water

A chaotic water effect is not always appropriate in a patio, where noise can echo and reverberate, as a result aggravating you and your near neighbours. But using the basic cascade principle, you can achieve a gentle fall of water.

If water flow is reduced and then released in a broad sweep along the top edge of the wall, it will flow down slowly, hugging the vertical surface. This water curtain concept translates very well to a free-standing screen made of polished steel or translucent glass. It would make a magnificent visual conclusion to a long, narrow canal or a striking centrepiece for a formal terrace.

Right: This dream pool extends right through to the house, creating a smooth visual transition between inside and out.

Shaping Water

Water moves smoothly over polished surfaces, making steel, marble and stone suitable candidates for a range of different water features.

Spheres and globes provide a sculptural opportunity that can be adapted in a variety of ways to suit the needs of your garden space. The curved form offers an effective way in which to combine an attractive shape with a beautiful material, allowing water to bubble up through a vertical tube inside. Spheres work very well in a shallow pool or in a small

container of water that can be placed easily in a confined area. A large, silvery sphere would look mysterious as it seemed to rise out of a still pool, while a group of granite balls would make a striking feature in a paved area, with the reservoir and pump concealed in a container somewhere under ground.

The Lure of the Swimming Pool

In hot climates, swimming pools will often dominate the entire patio. Inside-out concepts allow pools to merge with the house, while plunge and lap pools are combined with shady, terrace verandas.

These ideas can be borrowed and adapted in cooler climates. A warm plunge pool or relaxing jacuzzi, ideally solar-heated, can usually be accommodated.

Safety note: *Children should be supervised at all times when near water. If you have an open-air pool consider security fencing, surface covers, alarms and motion detectors.*

Left: *Three tall steel cylinders spout freely to create a dynamic backdrop to a still pool.*

MAKING A STEEL WATER FOUNTAIN

This stylish and contemporary water feature is made from three stainless-steel tubes. The water tumbles from slits near the tops of the tubes, as well as overflowing from the tops and running down the sides. A steel fabricator should be able to supply standard stainless-steel pipes. The ones pictured here have slots cut with a hacksaw 5–10cm (2–4in) from the top of each pipe and each one is fitted with a baseplate for stability.

1 Clear and level a dish-shaped area to a depth of about 5cm (2in). In the middle, dig a hole to accommodate a plastic reservoir. Use a qualified electrician to set up a power supply, an outdoor socket or waterproof junction box.

2 After fitting the reservoir and ensuring that it is completely level, backfill around it with soil or sand. Line the cleared area and reservoir with geotextile fleece or sand. Cut a hole in the fleece over the reservoir.

3 Lay pond liner over the fleece and reservoir. Gradually add water to the reservoir to pull the liner into place. Stand the stainless-steel pipes on top of the liner next to the reservoir, making sure that they are vertical.

4 Place the pump in the reservoir, covering it with a galvanized metal grille. Cut a hole in the grille for the pipe to pass through. Then, to keep back finer particles, cover the grille with fine plastic shade netting.

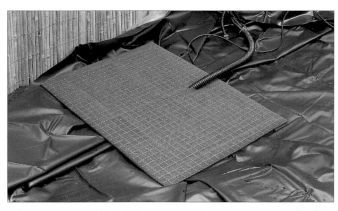

5 Connect up a 2.5cm (1in) hose to the pump, securing it with a clip, and connect the other end to a three-way T-piece.

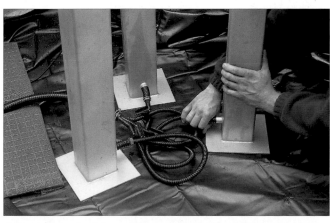

6 Connect each of the outlet pipes to a 1.3cm (½in) hose and flow taps. These are then, in turn, connected and secured with clips to the inlet pipes on each of the steel tubes.

7 Before completing the installation, test the water flow rate and make adjustments as required. Cover the floor with cobbles and rocks, concealing the hose and taps. Turn on the power.

LIGHTING FOR A MODERN SPACE

Contemporary lighting ranges from functional low-level path and step lighting to works of art. Minimalism characterizes the design of most modern fitments, although softer, organic and abstract forms have inspired some outdoor light sculptures. And while the look of contemporary lighting is usually quite sophisticated, there is room for lightening the mood with fun and quirky effects.

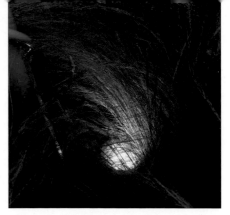

Above: *A red uplighter among feathery* Stipa tenuissima *looks like glowing embers.*

Left: *Low-level recessed spots cast sufficient light for safety while highlighting various architectural elements and establishing a chic ambience.*

Metallic Lights

Wall lights, including pendant designs and uplighters, might be made from polished or brushed steel, copper or ceramic. The sleek shapes add sculptural interest to the modern patio garden and you can sometimes find other lighting elements, such as pathway or stairway lights, in the same design.

If you want to mix and match light fittings, it is usually best to pick ones made from the same material or that have some other element of conformity. Alternatively, combine very simple models, such as slender post lights, bulkhead lights, brick and paving block lights and metallic recessed lights. The latter, made with steel and chrome fittings, are unobtrusive and blend easily with decking boards and brick or rendered walls.

It is useful to consult a qualified lighting engineer at the beginning of any building work, as integrated lighting requires proper planning. White or coloured LEDs are extremely long-lived, making them ideal for less-accessible recessed fitments. Consider adding extra interest by using dichromatic or multicoloured units.

String and Rope Lights

With the advent of LEDs, outdoor fairy lights, or string lights, have become increasingly popular and specialist lighting firms offer a wide range. These include flower, fruit and leaf designs, insects and birds as well as more eccentric subjects. Simple neon-blue or white strings add a more romantic note to seating areas than fixed wall or recessed lights, and strings with

bunches of chilli peppers, for example, could enliven a small dining area on a roof terrace.

Another option for hi-tech patios are rope lights with clear plastic tubing containing lines of coloured lights. This flexible lighting can be wound into a sculptural form and lights can be programmed to give either a static display or a gradual fading from one colour to the next. Avoid the frenetic light-switching programmes.

Coloured Floods

When fitted with tinted covers, small halogen floodlights, or minifloods, as well as spotlights allow you to colour-wash walls and trees.

Above: *Built-in lighting magnifies the dynamic effect of these water jets and extends the drama of the torch flares.*

You can totally transform the look and energy of a garden at night by adding colour to fine metal mesh or glass brick screens, or to garden buildings and pale rendered walls. And in winter, especially, coloured light can make the most of the sculptural qualities of a bare, deciduous specimen tree.

The Cutting Edge

Specialist lighting companies offer effects from stylish underwater lights to shimmering fibre-optic displays, and even light sculptures made from stacks of tempered glass.

Dichromatic and multicoloured units fitted with light-programming devices also allow you to change the mood of an area at the flick of a switch. More avant-garde examples allow you to project images on to bare walls or use laser displays. But whatever lighting scheme you choose, make sure that it is energy efficient and installed by a qualified electrician. Switch off lights when they are not in use to avoid light pollution and annoying your neighbours.

Above: *Here a highly theatrical effect has been created using a mirrored wall running alongside a flight of steps whose risers have been lit with neon blue fibre-optic piping.*

LIGHTING A PATHWAY

Low-voltage LED lights cast a clear, white light, ideal for illuminating a pathway or flight of steps in a contemporary patio. Designs vary, but there are many minimalist styles including small, sleek post lights such as the ones illustrated. These are robust and have a long life, making them practical for use in the garden.

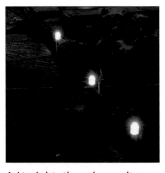

1 Push the spikes on each of the lamps into the ground, ensuring they are properly upright. There is usually plenty of cable between each unit to allow you to set them at the desired distances.

2 Use a trowel to dig a shallow channel along the edge of the pathway and then bury the low-voltage cable under the soil. Tuck the cable in neatly to avoid accidental damage.

3 The lights are partially camouflaged by the planting during the day, and they are fine to use in all kinds of locations around the garden in conjunction with hard or soft landscaping.

4 At night, these low-voltage lights cast a soft glow over the pathway, adding not only to the garden's safety, but also helping to create an appealing ambiance for however you use the area.

MAINTAINING YOUR PATIO

Whether you are a regular or occasional gardener, time outdoors among the plants is refreshing and restorative. Patios tend to be easy to maintain. Often there is no lawn to cut or large hedges to trim. And, with raised beds and containers, heavy work such as digging may not be necessary. Even watering can be done automatically. However, regular feeding of plants in pots and planters and feeding the soil is essential.

Touching up paintwork, treating wood, ensuring borders and paving are weed-free, and regular deadheading, will keep your patio spick and span. In a limited space, careful pruning, shaping and supporting of plants becomes especially important, and spring is a busy preparation period. Once autumn arrives, the focus turns to sweeping up fallen leaves, protecting tender plants, patio furniture and terracotta pots from the coming winter. Pools, pumps and filters also need attention.

Left: *A patio display such as this will need daily nurturing, and once or twice a year the patio should have a thorough spring-clean.*

PLANT UPKEEP

In a small garden, essential regular maintenance should include supporting plants and tying in shoots, removing faded blooms and investigating yellowing leaves. With good, fertile soil you may grow strong, healthy plants with plentiful flowers and fruits, but patio gardens often have poor, impoverished ground and plants need additional help in the form of feeding and mulching.

Above: *Climbers need different levels of support. Clematis prefer a wire lattice.*

Above: *Cut off unwanted stems and check that existing ties aren't too tight.*

Above: *Creating a framework of stakes and twine will give a plant extra support.*

Above: *When a mass of flowers goes over, such as marguerite daisies and lavender, use hand shears to deadhead them.*

Supporting Plants

Herbaceous perennials, herbs and lax shrubs may need support and this is best added as new shoots start to come through, so that the underlying support structure is eventually camouflaged. Support ranges from pushing in a few twiggy sticks to create a framework of stakes and twine or using purpose-made climbing frames, wall trellis or wires. Climbers and wall shrubs produce numerous new shoots and you will need to select the ones you want to keep and train and tie these on to their supports. Fan the stems out or train along horizontal wires to stimulate increased flowering and fruiting. Don't pass stems behind trellis panels or wires; rather tie them on to the front of the support. This ensures much easier maintenance.

Deadheading

This process prevents plants using up their valuable resources by setting seed. It also tricks the plant into producing more blooms in an effort to reproduce, and so

Above: *For large rose heads, cut back to the stalk base or just above a joint.*

Above: *Plants rarely recover a good, natural shape after having collapsed in the wind and rain, so early support is essential.*

lengthens the flowering season, especially for annuals. There are several ways to deadhead depending on the plant (see pictures below). Leave some sculptural seed-heads for autumn and winter decoration.

Above: *Once faded, small blooms may be pinched out between finger and thumb.*

Feeding

Regular feeding, especially when flower buds are developing and plants are in bloom, is essential. Check fertilizer packets to find the right balance for your flowering or foliage plants as well as for crops in the productive garden. Nitrogen (N) makes leafy growth, phosphorous (P) develops roots and potassium (K) promotes flowering and fruiting. These are expressed as an N:P:K ratio.

If you are looking for a feed for leafy vegetable crops, for example, you would choose one with a relatively large amount of nitrogen.

Just as with a good multivitamin tablet, you will also see additional trace elements listed on packs and bottles, including iron, manganese, and boron. These additional nutrients can help ailing plants suffering from deficiencies in their diet, which show up as discoloration of leaves and other abnormalities.

Tomato feed, which is high in potassium, works well on sparsely flowering plants producing leaves at the expense of bloom, while rose fertilizer is a tonic for other flowering shrubs and climbers, such as clematis and hydrangea. Use specially formulated ericaceous feeds for plants that need to grow in acid soils. And before the foliage of spring bulbs and lilies starts to fade, build flowering reserves using a high potash feed.

Above: *High-performing displays in containers and small raised beds need regular summer feeding. Nutrients are limited due to the small soil volume.*

Above: *Weekly liquid feeds between mid-spring and late summer are best, but top dressing with a granular, slow-release fertilizer in spring and midsummer suffices.*

Above: *Some fertilizers can be mixed with water from a hose and simply sprayed on to plants. This saves time and avoids heavy watering cans.*

Top Dressing

Using well-rotted manure, spent mushroom compost and garden compost (soil mix) for top dressing conserves moisture and improves soil texture and fertility. Apply the mulch thickly (8–10cm/3–4in) deep) in autumn (fall) or late winter on to moist soil, keeping it away from the stem bases to prevent rotting.

Rejuvenating Plants

Some quick-growing herbaceous plants and established bulb clumps may become overcrowded, causing poor flowering. To rejuvenate, lift and divide in autumn or spring (or, in the case of spring bulbs, after flowering). Improve the soil and replant the smaller vigorous portions, discarding the old, congested centre.

Plants in pots should be replanted into a larger container before they become pot bound to give the roots space to develop. If you want to keep a specimen in a specific pot, scrape off the loose top layer of potting mix and replace with fresh, adding slow-release fertilizer or a layer of organic mulch. If you can get it out of its pot, do so and scrape off loose compost from the root-ball. Cutting the mat of roots back slightly stimulates new growth. Ensure that compost (soil mix) is properly worked in down the sides of the pot.

Above: *Ease a pot-bound plant out, pushing through the drainage hole.*

Above: *Always feed after pruning shrubs and climbers to replace lost resources. Winter pruning can often be accompanied by mulching with manure or compost.*

Above: *Agapanthus is moved into a larger container without disturbing the roots.*

PRUNING AND TRAINING

A small garden that is planted with shrubs and climbers can soon look unkempt and overcrowded if regular pruning and training is not carried out. It is helpful to keep a diary of which plants need dealing with at particular times of year so that you don't inadvertently cut something back at the wrong time and spoil its flowering display or fruit production.

Above: *For best results prune wisteria in late summer and again in late winter.*

Left: *Mock orange (*Philadelphus*) and other spring and early summer flowering shrubs are pruned back once flowering is over.*

Right: *The thorny stemmed evergreen firethorn (*Pyracantha*) can take up a lot of room and is best when espalier trained.*

When to Prune

Long-lived shrubs and trees, such as magnolias, Japanese maples and evergreen azaleas, are slow growing and need little pruning. Fast-growing shrubs, and ones that produce an abundance of flowers and fruit, are often short-lived. Examples include buddleia, broom (*Cytisus*), lavender, and shrubby mallow (*Lavatera*).

If you can't judge when to prune fast-growing deciduous plants, it is usually safe to cut out around a third of the oldest stems in spring. A good guide is to prune plants that flower before the longest day of the year just after flowering, and to prune those that flower after that in the spring.

The first group includes spring and early summer-flowering shrubs, such as mock orange (*Philadelphus*). Remove a large proportion of the flowered wood and leave newer shoots to mature the following year.

The second group includes buddleia and late-flowering clematis. Prune these back to a framework of branches as they have time to produce mature wood.

You also need to cut out damaged or diseased wood and old or unproductive branches on flowering or fruiting shrubs and climbers.

Fruit Bushes and Trees

After harvesting soft fruit such as raspberry and blackberry, prune old canes out and tie new ones into supports. Most bush fruits are pruned after harvesting to maintain an open shape. Many can be trained to save space. Shaped and trained apple trees are normally pruned twice a year – once in midsummer and again in winter. Follow individual pruning requirements, as timings vary.

Above: *It is often easier to prune bare branches in the winter or spring as you can easily see what needs to come out.*

Above: Hydrangea paniculata, *when pruned strongly, will produce large and well-formed flowers.*

Above: *Prune bush and patio roses hard back in late winter. Remove dead, diseased, weak or crossing branches.*

WATERING TECHNIQUES

Watering can be tricky in patios. Not only do house and boundary walls create a rain-shadow effect, but there may also be little exposed soil for water to drain into. The amount of plants growing in a small plot can also put a strain on resources. And if you are growing mainly in pots and raised beds, some form of automated watering system could be very useful.

Above: *Divert water run-off from paving directly into borders to keep them watered.*

Conserving Water

Once established, plants should need watering only during periods of drought. Newly planted specimens, especially shrubs, need watering throughout hot, sunny or dry spells in their first year.

On free-draining, sandy soil or when gardening in containers and raised beds, focus on drought-tolerant plants. You can mulch with moisture-retentive organic materials, such as bark, well-rotted manure and garden compost, to seal in moisture.

Don't water overhead using a hosepipe and avoid short bursts of general watering. Use a watering can in the cool of the morning or the evening to reduce evaporation.

Hand and Automatic Watering

If you are away for more than a few days at a time in the summer, a willing neighbour or an automatic

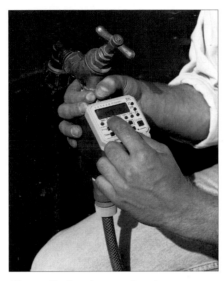

Above: *Setting the watering times on an automatic watering system.*

watering system is essential. Such a system can be efficient if it is properly adjusted and monitored. Most automatic irrigation systems include special accessories for watering wall containers, baskets and patio containers, and they are easy to put together or extend.

Water Capture

Provide a ready supply of rainwater by running the downpipes from the main house roof into water butts.

You can buy butts designed for fitting into confined spaces. Plastic water butts aren't the most attractive but you can camouflage them using trellis covered with climbers.

When building a garden, ensure that the paving slopes slightly to direct water into beds and borders, especially in low-rainfall areas and where the soil is free-draining. You can also divert rain from guttering into the beds if the flow is not too great.

Above: *When watering small plants and seedlings, use the watering can's rose fitting, otherwise the flow of water will disturb the soil and may uproot plants.*

Above: *A simple system for newly planted borders, as well as beds used for crops, is a leaky or perforated hose attached to an outdoor tap.*

Above: *Trellis screens in position around a butt, ready to be planted up with attractive climbers.*

Above: *A hosepipe with various attachments can speed up watering and make it easier to reach wall containers and baskets.*

SEASONAL JOBS

Small garden spaces demand careful upkeep because your attention is focused within that confined area and everywhere is on show. Many general maintenance jobs can be done in a matter of minutes and could become part of your daily or weekly routine, along with watering and deadheading, but once a year it is good to have a really thorough spring-clean.

Above: *Spring brings many maintenance tasks, but don't forget your spring flowers.*

Spring

The dead remains of many plants, including ornamental grasses, are still looking attractive in the spring. In early spring the dead material pulls away easily. Now is also the time to deal with overwintering weeds or annuals that may have sprouted.

Once the border is tidy, top dress with well-rotted manure or garden compost (soil mix) to get plants off to a good start, or refresh worn areas of mulch to keep down weeds.

Once spring is here, sub-shrubby specimens, such as penstemon and Russian sage (*Perovskia*), will show signs of new growth on their lower stems. Cut back the old woody growth to just above where you can see regeneration taking place.

Use the warmer days of late spring and early summer to retouch exterior paintwork and apply wood stains to freshen up fences and trellis.

Scrub unwanted algae and mud splashes from the base of rendered walls, garden statuary and bird baths and hire a power washer to lift algae, moss and grime from porous paving.

Summer

During summer, give hardwood furniture at least a couple of coats of teak oil, or re-apply exterior varnish or paint. Treat wrought- and cast-iron furniture with a rust-proofing paint after removing loose flakes with a wire brush and/or power washer.

At this time of year top up water levels in ponds and take action if blanket weed becomes a problem or if oxygenating plants are becoming too vigorous. Pull out excess weed and compost it. Water lilies and marginal plants should be thinned as necessary.

Autumn

Falling autumn leaves should be cleared frequently to prevent them smothering delicate plants and making surfaces slippery. If you have room to make leaf mould (a good soil conditioner), pack leaves into a perforated refuse sack and store them in a shady corner for a year.

If your garden has lots of autumn leaf litter, cover pools and ponds with netting to prevent leaves fouling the water. Before icy winter weather descends, clean and maintain pond pumps and filters. You may need to lift them for dry storage over winter.

Winter

Over the winter months, protect wooden and metal furniture using waterproof fabric covers. If possible, move wooden chairs and tables into a shed or summer house, because covers can cause condensation, which damages the timber.

Terracotta pots and ornaments are vulnerable to frost damage, so move them to a sheltered corner, take them under cover or protect them *in situ* using bubble plastic insulation or hessian stuffed with straw.

Pond pumps and filters should be switched off for winter as fish or amphibians survive in zones of warmer water, and the activity of the pump mixes warm and cold together. Prevent freezing by using an electric de-icer or by placing a floating plastic container in the water.

Above: *Treat woodwork and trellis panels to a fresh coat of paint or stain in the spring or early summer.*

Above: *Decaying leaves look untidy and can become slippery in the wet, so sweep them up regularly.*

Above: *Top up ponds and features running from small reservoirs, as required, to protect the pump.*

PLANT PROTECTION

In the sheltered confines of a patio garden you may be tempted to grow all kinds of tender plants. Although they may thrive during the summer, keeping them alive in winter can be more difficult. Plants in containers are particularly vulnerable. However, don't worry if you don't have a greenhouse or conservatory. It is possible to protect many plants where they stand.

Above: *Provide extra protection for tender wall shrubs such as* Ipomoea hederacea.

Protection from Frost

Some of the worst damage to soft new growth is caused by late spring frosts. Plants most vulnerable to frost are soft woods, bloomers that are still growing and potted plants. Frost can have a devastating effect on the flowering of *Hydrangea macropylla* cultivars (mophead and lacecap hydrangeas). Japanese maples, camellia and pieris are also vulnerable. The greatest threat of frost is during the night when the temperature drops enough to freeze the moisture on plants. Signs of frost damage include darkened, yellowed or mushy leaves or leaf curling. So if frosts are forecast protect the flower buds and shoot tips by draping the plant. You will need to attach horticultural fleece or bubble plastic to a horizontal batten temporarily fixed above the plant. Stretch the fabric over the plant and secure it at the base with a heavy piece of timber or a few bricks. Alternatively, tie the fleece over the plant using pegs or string. Mulch the base of the plant with bark to protect its roots.

Mulching Border Plants

Tuberous plants and bulbs can often be protected in the border simply by applying a thick bark mulch. However, take care not to pile this material up against the base of shrubs, climbers or semi-woody plants, as the accumulated moisture can cause rot. In many regions, dahlias and canna (Indian shot) can be left in the ground rather than being lifted and stored.

House and Conservatory (Porch) Plants

Houseplants, orchids and cacti kept in the patio garden for the summer should be moved back indoors in late summer or early autumn before night temperatures fall too far. Before doing this, give each plant a thorough check and search for aphids and other pests, such as slugs and snails. Tender fuchsias and marguerites, as well as potted figs, can stay outside a little longer, but they must be brought in before the first frosts. Don't overwater at this time. Figs can be stored in the darkness of a garage or cellar once leaves have dropped.

Tender bulbs and tubers, such as begonias, lifted for the winter, need not take up a lot of space and can be overwintered in a frost-protected coldframe, garage or shed. Store them in barely moist compost (soil mix), checking for pests, such as vine weevil, or evidence of rot beforehand.

PLANTS TO WINTER WRAP

- *Astelia chathamica* (silver spear)
- *Callistemon* species and cultivars (bottle brush)
- *Cordyline australis* (cabbage palm), red-leaved and variegated forms
- *Ensete ventricosum* (Abyssinian banana)
- *Eriobotrya japonica* (loquat)
- *Hebe* (large leaved cultivars)
- *Leptospermum scoparium* cultivars (manuka, New Zealand tea tree)
- *Metrosideros excelsa* (Christmas tree)
- *Musa basjoo* (Japanese banana)
- *Myrtus communis* (myrtle)

Above: *Cluster vulnerable container plants together against a warm wall to give them added protection.*

Above: *Protect tender bulbs and perennials* in situ *by heaping on dry leaves, bracken or bark.*

Above: *Use fleece to prevent frost damage to flower buds and tender shoot tips on magnolia and hydrangea.*

INDEX

ACKNOWLEDGEMENTS

The publishers would like to thank the following for the use of their gardens for photography: Jane & Geoff Hourihan; Peter & Murie Sanders; Leslie Ingram; Jim Austin & Jenny Patel; Martin Faultless; Barbara Williams; Bellamont Topiary; Capel Manor; & the Baron of Cam'nethan. Thanks also to the designer Alan Gardner, who was so generous with his time and introduced us to various locations, some his own designs (see Baron of Cam'nethan's garden on pages 124bl and 125tr); also to Vivienne Palmer, who set up & modelled the sequences on pages 27, 37, 39 & 133; & to Richard Sutton who set up and modelled those on pages 89, 95 & 135. Thanks to Finnforest UK who gave us the screens to use in the sequence on page 135.

The publishers would like to thank the following designers and institutions for allowing their gardens to be photographed: **New Zealand** p10m and p82t Gordon Collier's garden; p26bl Karaka Point Vineyard; p48br Hamilton Botanic Gardens; p64tr Monterey House; p71 design Tim Durrant; p83t Sarah Frater; p86m Neudorf Vineyard; p92bl Larnach Castle; p112t Bibby garden; p114tr Mincher; p119tr Waitati Garden; p120bm Rapaura Water Gardens; p137br Otari-Wilton's Bush. **The Hannah Peschar Sculpture Garden** p25tr Black & White Cottage, Ockley, Surrey, garden design Anthony Paul, stoneware design Jennifer Jones. **Chelsea Flower Show 2004** p112bl The

Japanese Garden Society, design Maureen Busby. **Chelsea Flower Show 2007** p42t Casa Forte, design Stephen Firth & Nicola Ludlow-Monk; p75t The Fleming's & Trailfinder's Australian Garden, Fleming's Nurseries, design Mark Browning; p126–7 The Amnesty Garden, design Paula Ryan & Artillery Architecture; p129b The Westland Garden, design Diarmuid Gavin & Stephen Reilly. **Chelsea Flower Show 2008** p83br Real Life by Brett, design Geoffrey Whiten; p48bl Spana's Courtyard Refuge, design Chris O'Donoghue; p70bl The Children's Society Garden, design Mark Gregory; p89tr, p92t & p141bl The Dorset Cereals Edible Playground, design Nick Williams-Ellis; p86br & p90m The Summer Solstice Garden, design Del Buono Gażerwitz; p96br Shetland Croft House Garden, design Sue Hayward; p125t Garden in the Silver Moonlight, design Haruko Seki & Makoto Saito; p132br The Pemberton Greenish Recess Garden, design Paul Hensey & Neil Lucas; p136m Gavin Jones Garden of Corian, design Philip Nash; p140m The LK Bennett Garden, design Rachel de Thame; p142m Fleming's & Trailfinder's Australian Garden, design Jamie Durie. **Hampton Court Palace Flower Show 2007** p30bm The Ruin on the Corner, design Keppel Designs; p35tl Learning to Look After Our World, Alton Infant School; 36b Silver Glade, design Chris Allen & Dorinda Forbes; p131tl Full Frontal, design Heidi Harvey & Fern Alder; p131tr In

Digestion, design Tony Smith; p144m The Raku Garden, design Rachel Ewer. **Hampton Court Palace Flower Show 2008** p62b Living on the Ceiling, Warwickshire College; p70br & p108 Holiday Inn Green Room, design Sarah Eberle; p72t Formal Elements, design Noel Duffy; p76b The Burghbad Sanctuary, design David Cubero & James Wong; p104m The Widex Hearing Garden, design Selina Botham; p111t Three in One Garden, design Lesley Faux.

The publishers would also like to thank the following for permission to reproduce their images. **Agriframe:** p96t; **Alamy:** p30br JHP Travel; p88tl Elizabeth Whiting & Associates; **Art Archive** p59 Bibliothèque des Arts Décoratifs, Paris; **Amy Christian:** p64tl; **Corbis:** p88b Eric Crichton; p124bl Arcaid; **Felicity Forster:** p69t; p75t; p89tl; p104t; p129b; p131tl; p131tr; p144m; **Garden Picture Library:** p29bl Clive Nichols; p31b Steven Wooster; p38m Juliet Greene; p40bl Lynne Brotchie; p45r Janet Seaton; p46b Philippe Bonduel; p47t Mark Bolton; p47b Juliette Wade; p65t Botanica; p72br Dominique Vorillon; p117t David Dixon; **John Feltwell/Garden Matters:** p59tl, p59tm, p59tr; **Garden World Images:** p14b J. Need; p41b A. Graham; p58br Mein Schoener Garten; p77b P. Smith; **Harpur Garden Images:** p23t; p46m; p68bl; p78b; p118 br; **Istock:** p68br. **Les Jardins du Roi Soleil:** p16tr. l = left; r = right; t = top; b = bottom; m = middle.